MW01711373

AFTER TRUTH

AFTER TRUTH

Explorations in Life Sense

Mervyn Sprung

State University of New York Press

Published by
State University of New York Press, Albany

Printed in the United States of America

For information, address State University of New York
Press, State University Plaza, Albany, N.Y., 12246

Production by Diane Ganeles
Marketing by Bernadette LaManna

Library of Congress Cataloging-in-Publication Data

Sprung, Mervyn.
After truth : explorations in life sense / Mervyn Sprung.
p. cm.
Includes index.
ISBN 0-7914-1703-4 (hard : alk. paper).—ISBN (invalid)
0-7914-1404-2 (pbk. : alk. paper)
1. Ontology. 2. Experience. 3. Rationalism—Controversial
literature. 4. Life. I. Title.
BD311.S65 1994
111—dc20 92-45189
CIP

10 9 8 7 6 5 4 3 2

CONTENTS

Preface vii

The Explorations

Inner and Outer 1
How Inner and Outer Arise/1
Interdependence of Inner and Outer/4
Vivial Exploration/8
Two Poles of Sense/11

Space 15
Space as Reality/15
The Everyday/16
Space and the Objects in It/20
Movement/24
Home of Human Worth/25
Mask of the Boundless/31

Time 37
Clocks and Calendars/37
Iz, Waz, To-Be, in the Now/42
Behavior and Iz, Waz, To-Be/47
The Non-Now/55
Now and Non Now Integrated as Story/59

Words 67
How Do We Live with Words¿/67
How Do Words Function for Us¿/75
Sense as Life Sense/80

Knowing 85
Is Knowing Unintelligible?/85
The Everyday/86
Knowing and Reality/89
The Family of Knowing/94
Knowing and Behavior/97
Western Science and Other Traditions/100
Knowing and Rationality/104
Knowing in Our Time/107
Knowing and Person/110

Person 113
Our Person/113
Possible Persons for Vivial Exploration/115
The Sense of I/117
The Sense of Me/119
I and Me: Phantoms/121
I not the Seat of Freedom/124
Self/127
Nietzsche's Life-Body/129
Body/130
Kant and Self/133
The Sense of Own/136
Aware Behavior/137
Individual and Society/143
The Discovery of Person/144
Person as Touchstone of Life/147

Vivial Sense 151
Exploring Vivial Sense/151
The Ur-Need for a Sense of the Way of Things/166
Traditions and Thrall/170
Thralls East and West/174
Vivial Sense and the Sense of the Way of Things/176
Nietzsche/178
Science/181
Sense of the Way of Things as Life Drama/182
Source/183

Name Index 185

Subject Index 187

PREFACE

It has become decisive for us to realize clearly in what way the thought tradition originating in Greece and Rome and developed in modern Europe and America is singular among classical traditions as we know them. All human reflection is a search for a way of making sense of human beings and the world they live in. The Western tradition is singular in seeking that sense in the form of a truth and through the power the Greeks called *nous*; Romans, *ratio*; and we in English, mind, intellect, reason. In the West truth and intellect have been inseparable, making theory the one and only form an understanding of ourselves and our world could legitimately take. Even a modest study of other traditions—Indian, Chinese, and Japanese—startles one into the realization that for these the resolution of the human predicament was not looked for as rational truth but as a discipline of life sense; and was not pursued by the light of one dominant faculty but by a person whose perceptions, feelings, mind, will, and body were integrated into one life.

The Greek dream of *knowing* the truth of the cosmic order lasted only a relatively brief if uniquely brilliant time in modern Europe. As religion withdrew into the churches philosophy ruled the public domain uncontested. This separation of the religious sense from the pursuit of truth was at once the making and unmaking of philosophy—and religion. In the subsequent centuries the pursuit of truth through rational theory burned with such vigour that it finally undermined its own faith. Reason found it could give no reasoned grounds for being the source of wisdom. It became clear that belief in reason is as much a faith as belief in the integrated person. Philosophy's dominance was further undermined by its own children: mathematics and the physical sciences.

Reason was patently more fruitful in such spheres than in the pursuit of wisdom.

Even Hegel's heroic effort to remake rational theory into an embracing system of knowledge had to succumb to the discoveries of the earth and biological sciences and, as we now can see, to the ruthless assault on the fundamental presumptions of rational truth by Friedrich Nietzsche. In our own time philosophers have gradually relinquished the hope of establishing a true theory of the universal order using arguments sustained solely by reason. In its place the unquenchable curiosity of the mind has turned to specialized enquiries—logic, ethics, language, theory of science—and to exploring the limits of the postmodern individual. No one today would attempt a total theory of the way of all things through reason alone. The most original Western thinkers of this century—Heidegger and Wittgenstein—have recognized this explicitly and creatively. Each has shown new ways of penetrating the nature of things while disclaiming any longer to be engaged in philosophy.

It is best to say it plainly. Philosophy, as the pursuit of one reasoned truth, is no longer possible. That great dream is not for us. We can no longer believe that the ultimate truths of our world are commensurate with the human intellect. Loss of faith strikes both at once. If the intellect is impotent to sense the secrets of things, there can be no secrets for it. If there are no secrets the intellect will hardly be interested in discovering them. So long as the intellect is the sole arbiter we can have no humanly significant world, no cosmos. In its place we have made for ourselves a chaos. We have no way of being sure how to determine the best life for humans. We know neither up nor down. Religion in the West long ago gave up the attempt to embrace new ages. Science is dominant, our truth and our reality. And its vibrant offspring—our electronic technologies—are usurping the place of the natural world in our everyday lives.

Some time ago Carl Jung predicted that the Western overemphasis of rational powers would subconsciously generate a compensation in the rediscovery of the powers of feeling and intuition. He understood the increasing popular and scholarly interest in Indian, Chinese, and Japanese thought in this way. Whatever merit his theory has, it is so that Vedanta, Buddhism, Taoism, and Confucianism as we discover them offer established ways of making sense of the human world through self-aware behavioral disciplines. Indeed these sources awaken us to the *fact* of the uniqueness of the Western attempt to make theory the only reputable form in which a sense of the way of things can be expressed.

It is the mark of our time that, as never before, the wisdom of all classical cultures is alive and available for mutual study. Not just for scholarly analysis but for vivial learning back and forth across language and time. As yet India, China, and Japan know more about Western philosophy and science than we know about their life wisdom. But we will learn more—not to imitate but to test and explore. There are signs of this even now. Certainly the tidal rush of science is generating an undertow of reaction. It is becoming increasingly clear that science's great merit as a practical, commercial, and military endeavor does not offer humans a world they can live in. Indeed it stultifies the need for such a world. Nietzsche's earth values, the rescue of the whole person from brain and psychic states and body medicine, the increasingly intensive critique of science and its technologies are signs of the reaction. Above all we have the unrelenting sense that there is more to life than our intellects can discover.

Our chaos takes the form of being obliged to believe in a world that does not sustain the kind of being we are sure we are. It is an abyssal contortion. Is a human being the latest of the animal kingdom? A cultural artifact like a painting? Or a being who has lost its memory of the heavens? We are at a fork in the road: onward into the barren enthralment of scientific fact and technology, or down the road to self-discovery.

In a previous work, *The Magic of Unknowing,* I suggested that if we could free ourselves from the most elemental presumptions of philosophy and science—that ideas *are* their serene meanings, upper-class citizens free of lowly feelings; that behavior inhabits another world than rational theory; that thinking dare not be considered a form of behavior—then we would be free to see that ideas, feelings, and behavior are inseparable and that humans make their worldly way by *sensing,* not knowing, where to go, what to do, how to understand themselves. I suggested that aware behavior—the experience of an idea fulfilling itself vivially—could be a way of establishing beliefs that are beyond the reach of theoretical truth or untruth.

In *The Magic of Unknowing* I wanted to show how unfounded our everyday notions of the world are. Not merely to discredit them but to raise the possibility that in some form of life exploration we could open ways through the thick interweave of beliefs—that space and time are outside us and physically measurable; that the mind exists in passing states determined by brain activity; that the human being is an individual centered around I and me; that knowledge is our light and illuminates facts; that behavior is determined by one's choices; and most elemental of all, that we live in two worlds, one inner and one outer—that shape and constrain our thinking and imagining and experiencing. Only so can we keep open the great living spaces where philosophy and religion once moved regally. This is not to establish new truths—we can't—but to probe the regions where one day again humans might find themselves at home and again discover the full range of their nature.

In the present work I attempt a modest beginning. I explore some of the basic beliefs by which we orient ourselves in the world and survive there, not by distilling problems into theories but by attempting to *live* the beliefs explored. This, of itself, took the form of a soliloquy—and brought unexpected results. Our common beliefs are not sustained by our behaviors: the way we live them is not the way we have been taught to understand them. We live worths in space and time that lie far beyond the everyday reality of these and nullify the claim of our everyday understanding to be the truth. This vivial field is anthill labyrinthian and broken. The exploration initiates its course with the universal belief that each of us is the center of an inner world of feelings, ideas, memories, intentions, our personal home where we are our very own selves, and that we must survive in an outer world of things and people that is quintessentially not ourselves. We seem to need this belief, but if we explore it vivially it metamorphoses into a paradox that discloses how persons stand in their world.

That is where I set my spade in the *soliloquy* that follows.

INNER AND OUTER

How Inner and Outer Arise

It seems self-evident: every human individual has a private inner life and lives in an outer realm of things that is common to all. Reality comes to us in two halves: the one inner, the other outer. It is obvious when we say it. But how are these two realms held together, how held apart? They structure our world, true. But what draws the boundaries, if there are such? How is it that they come to set the stage for our living? We're guided by our sense of what is inner and what is outer. What is that sense? How does it arise? No subject and object theories, just the simple question, how do inner and outer come to be for us in our living?

My commonsense realist friends will be after me at once: give full weight to the universal human experience. What one sees around one, picks up, remakes, sells or buys or studies as an object of science announces itself as *not* oneself. So do other people, their natures and purposes. There can never be any confusion. What one senses externally and interacts with is "out there". It is object and antipode to what one feels and knows. This always belongs to a person, the subject; it can't be conceived of in any other way. It is inner. How could anyone put this universal experience in doubt? It is the reality all humans live in.

Daunting. But not conclusive. Commonsense realism will have to convince me that the individual human subject as the carrier of the inner, and the world of objects as the carrier of the outer are, not conventions, but realities, each indefeasible. It may be so. But a vivial exploration stands in the way of my agreeing.

How do inner and outer arise? How do they function in our living?

Well, they are not awarely there for us until our one world begins to pull apart. The naive everyday world need not be disjoined into inner and outer: it is predominantly, unconsciously "just there". Until it shatters. That day dad was stricken with a ruptured appendix did it. It allowed an outer world to arise for the first time. Doctors at the bedside, a tense and focused household, thought of death. One moment was enough. The secure boy's world broke open. A rush of sense came from "out there" toward and into "this here". The world rose up as what was outer, against me, and fear rose in myself—not in the world. The neutral, not-inner, not-outer world of brother and sister, parents, home, neighborhood, school, and church, hitherto as unfailing as the seasons and so not noticed, took on its own existence, became outer. But was no longer secure. At the same time a focus of sense, unknown till then, rose over against it—in myself. Oddly the one rush of sense struck in opposing directions. It moved the world "away from", even as it moved "into" a center of awareness I could not even call myself, not then.

Whether such a sudden rupture of the everyday is common or whether there is more often a slowly growing awareness of the radical otherness of the world around, the discovery will be initially open, undefined. It must be. It's just that feelings seem closer, more intimate, while things and other people move away into a remoter otherness. Each negating the other even while making it possible.

The first wonderful paradox: there was on that afternoon no explicit me as possessor of the feelings, nor a world of things and other people spread out in space as their cause. Space was not a factor and yet the radical opposition of inner and outer was experienced spatially; feelings were inner whereas dad, doctors, and household were outer. Space serving as the dimension of understanding a mysterious happening that was not spatial. There is no way we can locate feelings in space, and yet human beings can orient themselves in the world only by sensing their feelings as "here", whereas other people and things are "there". It's so obvious that everything must be in space that common sense remains blind to the paradox. And philosophers, acknowledging the incongruity, resolve it by affirming a dualism of realms or principles: the natural world composed of material objects in space and time, and the intellectual world of perception and reasoning, which they are sure is not in space.

This is tempting. But no metaphysics. It should be more helpful to explore further in our nonmetaphysical understanding of what the words "inner" and "outer" mean for us. That is, how we live each of the words. Inner brings to mind closeness, privacy, the protected, the vulnerable; suggests going inside, reaching for what is hidden and secret, what has depth, what is close to the source, what has explanatory power. Inner is where thoughts and acts of will originate. It is also the baffling, the impenetrable, the mysterious, what withdraws from our will to know, what lies close to the truth, but is unnamable. The inner is where I and me dwell, impalpable as they are.

All that, and no doubt more. Outer brings to mind a different world. Outer is not so much in space as it is itself spatial. It is public, and often says appearance or surface. It is the locus of hard fact, of objects, of clear knowledge; yet it needs something other than itself to account for it. It is determinate, subject to stable principles that describe the behavior of things, but give no answer to why they should be as they are.

Such is the evocative worth of the two words. How much more interesting inner is. Something is out of balance. Perhaps the outer can sometimes have its own inner.

Still the great everyday is for the most part neither explicitly inner nor outer, but is incipently both. We're so caught up in habits and purposes we have little use for the distinction, whether we're inwardly or outwardly absorbed. Successful thinking or fantasy or mediation are rarely aware of themselves as inner. Nor is successful craftwork rarely aware of more than its materials as outer. Awareness seems able to shift in varying degrees and in varying scope to outer or to inner. But let the craft person's habits break down, let the thinker balk at the nonsensical, let the poet become aware of the great gulf between what one feels one wants to say and the stiff lumps of words one must use, let the mediator return to the surface, and the simple oneness of things is shattered. The world draws apart into two opposing "spaces": the in-here and the out-there.

Mere psychology, the realists say. The outer space is real space, measurable and objective; my nonspatial inner "space" is personal and subjective, dependent on real space for its stimulus and content. Why flog the difference any further?

Well one reason would be to clear up the realist misunderstanding of what is at issue. It's not the difference between a material world governed by immutable laws and a conscious world centered around the notion of a person. That hasn't been discussed. At issue is becoming aware of the ways in which an outer world develops as the field of behavior for humans and of the ways an inner world develops where humans feel they belong as themselves. The Cartesian problem of a self-aware I opposed to an impersonal world of mechanisms is for the metaphysicians. Of course, for purposes of everyday living and science it's not only helpful but necessary to learn to see the outer world stripped of all attributes that would make it unpredictable and uncontrollable. And in the same way the inner world gradually becomes experienced as I, me, my own self. What in the end these two reductions are worth for us is a mighty question. And a question light years away from the traditional philosophical problem. At this point there's no way of saying how a sense of inner becomes wedded to a sense of I-me-myself, nor how outer becomes the fallen realm of the mechanical.

It's enough to observe how the senses of outer and inner arise for us, how mutable are their boundaries, and how twinned they are in their natures. Each is what the other is not. Neither has shown any enduring reality, as yet.

Interdependence of Inner and Outer

The idealist makes much of the difference. He wants the inner to be evidence of a transnatural being—a person. He could be justified in this, but nothing has turned up so far to support his view. It is so that the sense of I-me-myself brings a warmth, a light, an unplumbable depth to the inner that is the condition of knowing where home is in the world and of fruitful actions there. But that, by itself, doesn't support any theory of human beings and their world.

The realist is still unhappy. He wants the difference in essence between outer and inner to be accepted. Human sanity, and science, he reminds us, depend on the belief in an objective world immune to the wishes and will of humans. Material objects, earth and metals, wood and water, and their micro-components are given to us as indifferent to human experience. They are not experiences nor the content of some sense or other, but rock-hard realities. And we know them as they are—their weight, shape, physical composition, motion. The difference between outer and the contents of our consciousness is given, the realist believes. Even the obvious dependence of our knowledge of objects on our external senses—smell, taste, touch, vision, sound—does not deter her/him. But it should, for they are part of the mysterious bond that holds inner and outer together. The self-evident, indefeasible difference between inner and outer is the troublesome element in the realist objection. The outer does give itself as reality; the inner as individual subjectivity.

So the world presents itself to a certain attitude and curiosity. But there are so many other attitudes and casts of mind. Everyday realism ignores how much the subject gives to the object, for that is no part of everyday experience. It returns to us as if from the outer world. We see grass as green and apples as red. But other beings see other colors. Sound for us is only what can be heard by the human ear. Almost all other species hear sounds too highly pitched for us or too faint. Human perceptual experience contributes to the nature of what humans perceive as the outer world. Inner and outer support each other.

How much more do feelings and ideas contribute to the objects of feeling and thought. The object of love reveals itself as lovable to the enamored person. The object of thought—Einstein's principle of relativity—reveals itself only to the mind that can grasp it. Rousseau's experience with Vivaldi's choir of orphans and waifs makes a powerful point. Entering the convent in Venice he was desolated at the sight of the girls: smallpox, blindness, retarded features. But when they sang, the angelic voices revealed their gay and lovely natures. They became different persons for him—beautiful. Before he left he had nearly fallen in love with them. Or Pascal's conversion to Christianity. Only after he had come to believe in the saving potency of Christ could he make sense of the Christian account of the corruption of all nature through the fall of man and the singular place of Christ in human history. The believing mind comprehended.

Of course such stories will offend the tough minded. But they make the one simple point quite believable: the sensitivities and faculties of belief and thought are not separated from the objects of feeling, belief, and thought by an insurpassable barrier, however outer these may be. This will be equally true of our concepts of nature and the inexorable laws that reign there. Incomparably more complex, but the principle can be maintained: only so much of nature will become scientific object as the human mind has the power to comprehend. Nature at all times will be the mirror image of the mind studying it. The outer object will be what the human mind has helped to establish.

This will seem subversive, even dangerous, crowding humans into the prison of their fantasy. Is the real world not right there before us? Did Dr. Johnson not dash his foot against a stone that certainly was not in his mind? Can we not *see* subatomic particles darting about on video screens? Must one not be slightly mad not to recognize reality? One is held to be mad if one can not distinguish between one's fantasies and ideas that will survive in conditions outside one's control. Madness obliterates the difference between inner and outer. I don't believe I'm mad but the question is subtle. In some sense we must live in an outer reality. It's just that our everyday draws the line too widely around what is outer, unwittingly appropriating thereby much of what has been contributed by the subject, and too tightly around the inner. How to see both as interdependent in one lived world?

Whatever the metaphysics of this, we live in a reality of rock and earth, trees and water, and skies and wind, and beings, some of whom we recognize as being like ourselves, and of course human-made roads and automobiles and computers, and critics and bad air. That all this has to be accepted as indifferent to one's individual will is beyond question, even though what these things are is what they are in a human world. The net of our worded ideas is thrown over all things. That there is a great faceless embrace holding the world and ourselves together, that behind the overlay of our human experience articulated in words, there is the ultimate givenness of cosmos and human—though not in these words—must be accepted. But "reality"? We can't be sure what even that word covers over. Even "matter" is a word overlay; so with "being", "existence", "consciousness". Whatever we say, however basic, "the outer world exists", "consciousness exists", "material objects are real", we are dealing with our experiences of something that we can never know except in our experience of it. In the everyday we quite sensibly overlook this and believe that matter and consciousness are irrefragible givens, foundations on which we may erect our world. It is important to see that this holds for consciousness as much as it does for matter. Neither guarantees its own legitimacy or is a basis for accepting the other. It is enough to awarely live them. To see the consequences for vivial exploration. There is no compelling reason why the human must oppose, absolutely, the existence of "material bodies" and "centers of consciousness". They are the extremes of our best effort to make sense of the world we find ourselves living in and to make living in it a senseful undertaking. Nothing can take us behind the matter of objects or the outright miracle of consciousness that evanesces under the very fingertips of our introspection.

Against the common belief that ideas and feelings are transparent just because they are "in the mind", they bring analysis to a dead stop. What is this "mind" in which they are held to exist¿ Doesn't it come and go like a bird at the feeding station¿ What is its nature, what is it doing when there is no feeling, no sensation, no idea "in" it¿ Without an idea present to tell us, how could one know that¿ And what are ideas and feelings made of¿ What is an "event" in consciousness¿ If ideas and feelings are themselves conscious why would they need a mind in which to exist¿ To try to say what consciousness and its events are is like trying to catch a beam of light in one's hand: somehow it will always be on the hand, but outside its grasp. This is most frustratingly clear when we try to grasp "I" or "me". We have a strong sense of them, but can not say what they are, what they can be made of. Even in the attempt, a second I appears that is aware of the first I and tries to study it. We can be sure that both are present, but not how. We can observe our own reading of their behavior, but have no way of knowing what they might be apart from that.

Inner and outer force us to recognize the brute fact that the foundation of our experience is independent of the human will and impenetrable to the human mind. But this makes the scientist very uneasy. He or she must insist that reality is given to us to investigate. And of course the scientist should. But it is not easy for him or her to agree that what we come to know about the nature of things is, observed dispassionately, a complex of behavioral interactions with "nature" that allow us to foresee its course, to alter its course, to make it useful to humans. And then to elaborate this knowledge into explanatory theories. So successful are scientists in this—affecting everything from drinking water to space travel—that their theories have won our trust. Science has become nothing less than a faith—or superstition. It will be some time before another mythology replaces it.

Vivial Exploration

Back to the vivial. To explore what promises to yield a little life sense for our benighted existence is my furthest ambition. We accept most of our beliefs about the outer and the inner worlds from our habitual practices and concerns. We assume outer and inner are two realities, interactive of course, but each with its inviolable properties. After all the idea of a kilometer is itself not a kilometer in length; the enjoyment of the sunset is itself not the sun setting. The frustration of being kept waiting has nothing to do with the true lapse of time. The external not-us is accepted as a brute fact. We believe we live that way. Because of fixed space and time we can anticipate events and make them serve our purposes. We couldn't pass one day without them. Our legs wouldn't be able to find the ground without fixed space, nor could we bake bread without unvarying time.

These beliefs accompany us through the day. Without them we could hardly make a move. Especially in an intrincately mechanical and electronic habitat. The more our kind of science is applied to the necessities and pleasures of the day, the more dependent we become on an external, quantitative, outer surround. The paradox of scientific democracy raises its head: the more the individual human and his or her needs become primary, the less does society need this individuality; and the less human does it become. Our world is so intricate we can become as lost in it as Hans and Gretel. The outer is swamping the inner. Everyday bulging with deadlines, production quotas, marketing programs, and the seductive electronic aids to childbirth, memory, amusement, and "communication". All closing in on one from the outer. When is there time to live?

That it has not always been so is some comfort. Fishing, nomadic, and agrarian societies have another sense of the surrounding world and their own importance in it. They naturally develop a sense of oneness with the seasons and the powers of procreation and growth. That's for the anthropologists but it helps to realize that one need not accept the prevailing technological habits of one's time. It is in our power to explore our relations with the world and to make discoveries that free us into our own way of taking a stand in it. Even if it's not easy.

This much is straightforward. Seeing, hearing, and the other senses, and our feelings and thoughts are capable not only of reporting outer facts for our personal and business undertakings. They have the power—this is the turning point and the beginning of vivial exploration—of discovering qualities and worths in objects that we habitually accept as outer, but which by their nature can be there only for a conscious, value-sensitive human, for the inner realm. Only the eye can bring painting, sculpture, and architecture to life for us. We say we can *see* the subtlety of colors, the spirit of the landscape, the power of a poised figure, the elegance of a building; and mostly believe it. But what spatial dimensions have the qualities of subtlety, power, and elegance? How long or wide is the jabbing vitality of a Varley landscape? How much does the vitality weigh? Must it not be so that objects and colors though "outer" can carry the inner worth of nature's vitality? However often we assume it is out there in the painting? Baffling!

This is not merely an art gallery experience. Through the eye we subvert inner and outer in the everyday world, continuously and unawarely. Do I *see* the mood of my wife, just because I have learned to read her facial and body behavior? Is mood in space, with a size and shape? Hardly. Only face and body are in space. My sense of their significance is an inner experience. Bafflingly carried by a body in the spatial world. We move through every social situation seeing facial and body gestures and responding to our inner sense of what they are telling us. Though mostly we believe that sense is coming to us from the people we are with.

But it is not only vision of art objects and humans that so function. I see a lake, a spruce tree, the moon. We commonly say they are objects in space. Yet the dimensions of the lake, the height of the spruce, the distance the moon is from earth are not what I see at all. I look at the lake and enjoy its freshness or tranquillity; at the spruce and sense its solemn age; at the moon and feel a lyric melancholy regardless of dimension or distance. I can't generate these experiences myself. And yet they are not physical properties of the objects. What a mix up! Inner experience seems the property of spatial objects, and spatial objects seem to be at home in my inner. This confounds our intelligence, but not our faculty of making sense of things. We live in and by that strange relationship.

It must be so. How else would everyday visual happenings be possible? The priest genuflects and we "see" an obeisance to the deity. If we are of the faith. The Buddha statue has a raised open hand and we "see" him assuring us that there is nothing to fear. If we are of the faith. Others see only a hasty kneebend or an empty palm. It will be so with all the outer senses. It's so obvious. We say rancid flesh smells bad. We say a parsnip tastes sweetish. We say the touch of a beloved hand is soothing. Hearing is perhaps the most striking case of all. It's certainly the most improbable. Mere vibrations in the air, from whatever source—the human throat, the passing wind, or arriving automobile—are, after seen things, the most important events in our world. It is hard to find a sound that is neutral to our inner sense. Sounds seem to clothe themselves in our feelings effortlessly. Who can separate the sound of laughter from a sense of carefreeness or perhaps crudeness? Who can separate the sound of crying from a sense of concern or perhaps annoyance? The infinity of tone shades in the human voice, and each carries its own properties of boredom, pretentiousness, diffidence, persuasion, tenderness . . . , as may be. Musical tones must be the clearest case. Do we hear mere sounds—and then translate them into feeling experience? That's not the way it happens. Our response to the musical instrument *is* a feeling response. We don't separate the notes heard from our feelings. The notes themselves are vigorous, lilting, somber, sweet. It is as though we were listening to our own inner stirrings. The oneness is striking. Only for technical reasons would we listen to the sounds with our ear, if we can.

Two Poles of Sense

The realist is bearing down on me. Have you never heard of projection, he or she counters. The process is quite simple and removes all your baffling discoveries about the way we live in the world. Everyone understands the cause and effect relation of external stimuli—light rays, sound waves, materials touching taste buds and nerve ends—and the physical sense organs in the human body. The external stimuli produce definite effects in the sense organs that we then experience as sight or sound or taste or whatever. As the external object has importance for us so we learn to project that importance back into the objects. We ourselves perform the simple mystery you are insisting on. We overlay our personal feeling reactions on the objects which cause them. No lake was ever placid; only a human's feelings can be.

I understand. The realist prefers to accept the mystery of the oneness of the human world at the level of sense organs: *they* transmute a physical event into a human feeling. This is so far outside our comprehension that I suspect it's false; at least it's a fruitless reduction of the problem. It's not the way we make sense of things, not the way we live. It removes the most telling and valuable attributes of the objects and people in our world. And dignifies the bare bones remaining—matter and bodies in space as reality. This pits a hopelessly subjective human life against an impoverished, virtually valueless outer world. It tears in two jagged pieces the close interweave of life.

Of course the mystery remains. No question. But realism is not the only way to locate and define the human conundrum. Seeing the mystery as how human feelings can detect the real properties of things is preferable. It doesn't accept physical science as the one basis of understanding. It allows primacy to the way we must live with things, not to a theory about them. And it leaves the world as it must be if we are to continue to live meaningfully in it: one world embodying the full reach of the human sense of worth. It is a mystery. And I must find out what vivial exploration can tell me about it.

Perhaps inner and outer are becoming too dominant. After all they're just words. Are there two realms of being answering to them? So far the evidence says no. Are they just two names for one world of experience? Again no. We cannot separate them, but we mustn't obliterate their profound difference. However much of its felt experience inner yields to the outer world, it never loses the sense of inner. Whatever its content, explicit inner is unmistakable, as is the sense of outer. The innermost experience is a strong sense of I and me, of my very own self. It is the one pole of all experience. And the outer thatness of things—just that things *are*—is the opposite pole. Odd, but it seems that even the unspatial inner feels itself spatially removed from the outer. That is not a metaphor. It is a lived spreadoutness. Inner is in some sense indefeasibly spatial; and outer, as experienced, is indefeasibly inner. The details of this would be overwhelming. It's enough for now to note that the human world is not composed of two realms, each with its own inhabitants and laws. It's better to say there are two poles in one world, each presupposing the other.

Is it an argument for the primacy of inner and outer that some balance between them is widely used as a mark of mental health? Some of us dwell closeted in the familiar, intimate world of our own feelings and fantasies. We transmute outer events into our private language and become strangers in the outer world, paranoid. Others stride through their own feelings unfeelingly eager to lock horns with the real problem of the outer world. They can empty their personal life of all depth, mistaking the busy world of computers and dollars for themselves and becoming as hard and shallow as their office machines: loss of a sense of self. Is it an argument that giving primacy to external enterprises results in people thinking communication between individuals proceeds via external means—fax, video screens, printed words—in people thinking that each individual remains isolated unless linked by external means of communication? Is it an argument that to give primacy to a world fleshed out in human values makes interpersonal appreciation and understanding a natural human gift?

Yes. Worth is the strongest argument.

It's clear that our most elemental sense of reality—each one of us a private being surviving over against a public world—is not confirmed by the way we live. Our behavior presumes the opposite. We treat other people and the things of our behavior world, not as alien, but as clothed with all the qualities they must have for ourselves to live humanly with them. They are like ourselves turned inside out. This must be universal, if almost incomprehensible for us in a science society.

Our public reality—myth—of isolated inner lives and external world of physical bodies can be seen as the result, in part at least, of stripping off all qualities of things that cannot be calculated scientifically. Science has created a world for its own purposes—in the pursuit of truth. But the paradox: we don't live that way. We are wiser than our theories. The difficulty is that we can give no acceptable explanation of our ability to live as we do. But who would make life wait on theory?

So it will be. We live in one world with two poles of sense: an outer direction and an inner direction. The full range of perceiving, thinking, and feeling moves freely between the two indefeasible poles. We live in continuous intimacy—not "communication"—with other humans, where all things and happenings have the worth our life sense tells us they have.

This suggests its own way of taking existence. Everyday inner and outer could be taken as a kind of durable stage setting. Life would be enacted within its walls and doors again and again so long as we believe it to be the real world. But if transparenced, then seen as a set of beliefs blocking our view of a larger life behind it. Yet persisting in the human world, over and again to be seen through. As the only possibility of our discovering what it conceals.

That is presumptuous of course. Though less so, if what our stage setting conceals were another, though grander, stage setting.

S P A C E

Space as Reality

That is one "reality", or one elemental belief about reality, that did not sustain its claim and reputation to be such. But inner and outer are everyday categories, not scientific. The proven elements of reality—space, time, material objects, knowledge—that have been relentlessly debated through ages of philosophy and science must be really real, just as real as the accuracy of an aerial bomb. Else how could we guide such objects through space and time with the surgical precision of scientific knowledge?

Again the scientific realist has a great swell of common opinion for support. Space is the most unquestionable reality in our world. We just have to open our eyes to see it. Right. Yet Zeno showed the Greeks that space as an infinitely divisible material element is incomprehensible. And Nagarjuna showed his fellow Indians the hopeless paradoxes in the belief that a solid body could occupy successive points in space. Of course none of our elemental concepts is immune to the disease of internal contradiction. Space is not singular. In any case this is not decisive for me. It's the living worth of our beliefs that needs exploring. Theories are for the theorist. What is the point of asking philosophical questions if we no longer have the ability or will to offer philosophical answers?

There is point, though, in asking of any idea-word, basic or trivial, how do I *live* it? Into what experiences does it lead me? What is its sense? That is, what is its worth in working out one's sense of life? That sounds presumptuous; but not to ask, what can the exploration of space tell me about what goes unnoticed in the everyday so long as I haven't explored it? That's a fair question. If there's a way to ask it. Not whether space is more female than male; or if it can be conceptually clarified; or how mathematical theories of space affect the movement of solid bodies. No. Simply following the idea-word where it leads and learning what it can tell me about the sense of the way of all things in this impenetrable world we find ourselves in.

But what of the reality of space? That was the initial question. Though it began to fall apart as everything appeared to belong in the indefinable matrix of inner and outer. The realist insists that space is the possibility of there being an outer world. She or he can argue for the physical reality of space with convincing clarity. Space, she or he insists, is physical because we can measure it, because it is divisible, and because it is objective: identical for every man, woman, and child in creation. The realist and the idealists strike sparks. For them space can be the home of Being and is not to be sullied by Descartes's bodily extension or Newton's one-dimensional mathematics. Or it can be Kant's belief that space is merely a way of perceiving things, unreal for things themselves. The worth of space for our life sense seems a little feeble in the presence of these traditional convictions.

But realist and idealist have argued since forever. Metaphysical arguments have a way of being unfruitful. Exploration in a time after philosophy cannot be merely the play of concepts according to the rules of definition and valid inference. There are no grounds for trusting the play of concepts in isolation from the feelings and values that carry them and give them life. An effort to understand space, or anything else, remains mere theory if its bearing on our life sense is ignored. Of course we don't know how to explore vivially—we have no "method." But the need for it sits so unmovably on the heart that it must be tried.

The Everyday

That is a change of direction and of question: leave the reality of space marking time and ask, what can space tell about the way of all things, about life itself? If it can tell anything. The realist and the idealist will be looking over my left and right shoulders, for sure. But it will make no sense to begin a vivial exploration with physics or metaphysics. What have they to do with our sense of the way of things? It is the obvious, the many ways space moves in and out of our everyday lives that has the story. That means exploring, as is possible, any type of experience—perceptual, conceptual, emotional, as may be—to which space is integral.

How find space? Where is it? What a question. One can as easily ignore one's own breathing as overlook the ubiquitous intimacy of space. One breathes in space, one assembles a whole world in space, voices arrive through space, and so do thoughts. Space seems lifeless, but it is where our life is. We bathe in it continuously. Still, it's a real question: how do we become aware of space?

Isn't it primarily what is outside of us? what is vaguely "out there"? Aren't what is "outer" and what is "in space" naturally taken to be the same? Not only tables and chairs and trees and fields are in space; so is our neighbor, all of him, his clothed body, his smile, his gestures and voice when he argues, even his indefinable, brusque manner. All that is "out there" and so we assume it must be in space. It seems that everything outside oneself is in space. "Inner" space is not a common, explicit perception. As everything "in" "outer" space is taken to be material, so, in some imprecise sense and yet pervasively and strongly, space itself is taken to be material. Even the Buddhists classed space with other physical elements—fire, water, air—and took it as what separated solid bodies from one another. We too make space a physical element in our everyday reality. Space is the great enfolder, holding all corners of our earth and its mantle of stars in place, and all the galaxies too.

But the idea-word "space" is perverse. It is not only a physical element spread out endlessly around us, it takes on, as well, every size and shape of the finite. Space is not only the container, it is equally the contained, we believe.

The measured floor surface contained within the four walls of a house is sold or rented as space, calculated at so much per square foot. There is space between lines and words on a page; so much space is permitted between adjoining houses; there is space inside an oil drum, though usually the volume of what can be put into that space—so many gallons of oil—is a synonym for the space itself. The space inside a refrigerator is translated into so many cubic feet and marks the value of the refrigerator. Each of us confers reality on some conventional system of measurement. My visible reality is made up of feet and inches and miles of space. Others find meters and kilometers in space. Grandfather layed out his fields in chains, rods, and furlongs. Space becomes real in the quantities our habits dictate.

We live space as something that has its own reality, and the realist believes this establishes her or his view. It can't be merely a projection of the mind onto outer things, because it is real enough to avenge itself on anyone who might think that. Fat men get stuck in tight places; pianos will not go down narrow staircases; only so much firewood can be piled into a one-ton truck; an armful of books will fill or not fill a given shelf space. Our simplest everyday habits imply spaces of familiar and real dimensions: we lower ourselves into a chair without looking, roll over in bed without falling out, duck our heads going down old cellar stairs. We're adjusting to fixed spaces incessantly. We arrange furniture and pictures in the unchangeable dimensions of a room's space. We move about the same room in the dark, every step measured to fit the spaces between the solid objects, as we are able to remember their places. Isn't the skill of the blind person with her or his cane irrefutable proof of the objectivity of space? So it seems.

The realist reminds that any measurement of space is universally valid. A meter is the same in France as in China. This alone guarantees its objectivity. Personal feelings cannot alter spatial measurement. And all our senses present space as objective. The eye confers the title of "object" on anything it sees. The ear can trace a sound to its physical origin in space, and so may a smell be traced. It seems that space is given with the world we wake up to.

When we walk with our eyes open it is our legs that know the distance they are from the ground. And we judge accurately the spaces closed to or open to movement. How could we survive in motor traffic if we didn't? Those who don't, don't. That the English word space is related to the Latin *spatiari*, to walk, and *spatium* was a time interval, makes the closeness of space and movement pretty clear. After all, if we've forgotten the measuring tape, we measure spaces by paces, and the army sergeant major carries, or used to, a pace stick for measuring the space to be traversed by a soldier's pace.

The relationships of space, movement, and time open up some

beautiful metaphysical conundrums, from Zeno in Greece to Nagarjuna in India, but not now. Nonquantitative uses of space are more interesting. They are a solid part of our everyday sense of the reality of space. Space can measure effort: I jog one mile and Guy jogs ten, putting out ten times my *effort*; I planted five acres of pine trees last year, Walter planted ten, double my *effort*. While I paint one side of the house, Guy can paint two; he works twice *as fast* as I do. And space can measure social quality. A spacious house or a large farm indicate superior status. Once upon a time a big car meant a good car; now, perhaps, small bespeaks quality. Either way, the space measurements of the car stand for qualities that are not themselves spatial.

Space carries attributes so far removed from physical space that, in the everyday, we call them metaphors. Don't some people have large hearts, some small minds; don't some have a broad outlook, some a narrow; aren't some thoughts deep, others shallow; aren't some deals on the level, others crooked? And space can carry aesthetic values, obviously. Sculptured figures, or living ones for that matter, are—if we don't think too hard—as much in space as telephone poles. We say, "Look at the *power* in Rodin's thinker," or "Note the *coiled strength* of the Greek discus thrower!" As if power and strength were of one nature with the lifeless bronze or stone in space.

Again space naturally assumes personal or psychological attributes. Some spaces, like one's own study or workshop or living room, are havens in a raucous world. Others—convention centers and official residences—are chilling, lifeless, the very essence of "public." Enclosed spaces—cellars, clothes closets—can be frightening, as can open spaces—prairies or the ocean. Entire buildings can, as spatial objects, be elegant—the Taj Mahal "floats"; others are merely *Baukunst* functional. Churches and cathedrals enclose space, each in its own way. Westminster Abbey is a national sepulcher and shrine; the Cologne Cathedral lifts one's eyes and feelings up and up. And the church of St. Sofia, Istanbul, is space orbed serenely for the spirit. In each case there is so-and-so much cubic space, but the shape of the space transports it worlds away from cubic measurements. One might say that space wears the attributes of religious feeling easily.

Nothing is new in all this. Shades of the riddles of inner and outer. But it brings to mind some of the ways the word space fleshs out the world we live in while confirming our understanding of it as real. It seems that space is not separated from the way we live after all. Truth is that our behavior is wiser than our theories. In the everyday we allow spatial objects naturally to possess qualities that are, in our theory, not spatial at all. And remain happily unaware of the contradition.

We get by for the most part believing that our terms of spatial measurement—inches and feet, kilometers and light years—tell us quantities of space. But this is becoming suspect. It is a behavioral ellipsis, a natural belief, that the everyday has no occasion to falsify. It is a kind of benevolent illusion. Space does not present itself to be measured, only objects and distances do. And how quaint to think space exists in quantities precisely equivalent to any system of measurement. Miles are as seldom found in space as kilometers. However, space is behaviorally so pervasive it is reluctant to allow itself to be absorbed completely into the extendedness of objects and the distances between them. It ghosts about in the background, ungraspable but inexorcisable—if not as material and measurable.

Is space perhaps given with consciousness? Is it the openness of awareness itself, by nature unbounded? The groundhog, even the mole, are inconceivable without a sense of space, though it be of lesser range than that of migrating birds. Even if they make no conundrum out of space, as humans do, mustn't we believe that the enabling openness of their burrowed space is as much given with their consciousness as sky space is with our own?

Space and the Objects in It

Space, in our everyday behavior and talk, has many faces, that's clear. But one face has been reluctant to show itself: how space is related to the objects and obstructions that give our world the structure and measurements it assumes? The ancient Upanishadic thinkers thought it was fine material, all pervasive, bringing the truth everywhere on the wings of sound. What can we think? Is space what walls and ceilings enclose, or is it what encloses walls and ceilings, and all other things? Or is it both? Is it objects in space that are spatial, or is space spatial? Are perhaps the objects in space truly spatial, and space itself, being merely their absence, not spatial?

Can anyone answer such questions? Are they meant to be answered? Or just asked? That is the real question.

So, once again, what *is* space?

What about an ordinary solid object, like a wooden building stud, 2" × 6" × 8′. Is it extended in space? Well, it obviously is extended—8 feet in one direction, 2 inches in another, and 6 inches in a third. What about "in space"? What does this add? The piece of wood has a measured extension, but space doesn't offer itself to be measured, in addition to or apart from the piece of wood. As wood cannot be extended in any other way, why add the redundant "in space"? It suggests that space is a medium like water and should have some credit for allowing the stud to extend itself! That's not very persuasive, though we probably often feel that way.

And if we talk distances, there is the same redundancy. If the distance from Halifax to Vancouver is 4,000 kilometers we need never mention space; if the distance from one end of a wall stud to the other measures 8 feet, we need no mention of space either. Eight feet "of" space, 4,000 kilometers "of" space! That's absurd. Distance measures a linear dimension between two objects. Space has a thousand dimensions. It fractures language to say that distance is a quantity of space. And yet both extendedness and distance seem to need some added sense in the background to round out their full meaning. Is that a behavioral urge or a language expectation or a nagging absence of something? And distances and measured dimensions serve very well elliptically for functions that are not spatial: "How many two-by-six studs will I need for my house? Not more than 200." "How far is it from Halifax to Vancouver? About six days driving time." Space virtually vanishes.

What about cubic measurements? Do they measure space, or what fills space? It is too odd—impossible—to say, "a liter is a space 10cm × 10cm × 10cm in size." Does space come in sizes! And the word "volume" gets us nowhere. Is a liter a volume of space? Fractured language. Volume is defined by cubic measurement not by quantity of space. Usually it goes with the kind of liquid or solid whose volume is so measured. We have liters of gasoline or milk, and bushels of apples or wheat. Not liters or bushels of space. Does the word liter require the added notion of available space to make sense of it? Certainly not in the everyday; we have erased space from our awareness. It seems that cubic measurements usually define a volume of specific contents, not a volume of space. So neither cubic nor linear measurements measure space. That is sure. But space will not be crossed out of the puzzle. Our habit of presuming that linear dimensions, cubes, and distances are *of* space is strong. Is that an argument? Must space be presumed if they are to have their full meaning?

Does this help? Whatever cubic measurements we have reason to establish and whatever size we wish to construct solid objects, space is tolerant, space receives the human construct. Space offers no resistance even to heavenly bodies of unimaginable mass. Is that what space is: the possibility of unimpeded extension of objects and of unimpeded movement? Space defined through the absence of impediment? So be it. Because "empty" space is not empty of all matter, whether living or dead. Our feet and legs and the rest of us move "through space" when we walk, but that space is not empty. It is choked with oxygen, carbon dioxide, dust, plant pollen, industrial chemicals, bad smells, good smells, rain, snow—and how much else. Yet, so long as our bodies are unimpeded, we tell ourselves we are moving "through space", not empty space evidently, but still, for everyday purposes, the real thing. That is not precisely original, but its good sense strikes home for the first time. Does it mean that space has no structure of its own? That it is absence? That space is not "spatial"?

Odd, because as we live through our extended bodies, the everyday world seems to be a maze of "spatially" ordered objects and tasks and movements. The distance of the ground from the hips when walking, the spaces between cars and pedestrians in traffic, the space available when trying to park one's car, the rapidly diminishing distance of the landing track from the ski jumper as he descends, the position of the back when one wants to towel it, the movement of the other's hand when you reach out to shake it, putting food in one's mouth or brushing one's teeth, the location of the light switch in the dark, buttoning a coat without looking at the button holes—all this and our every move in the world presumes a "spatial" order in which we live and arrange, gratify our needs, and fulfill our obligations.

That's the way we commonly think, so there's some ground for it. But perhaps not the one presumed.

Kant's view, that space is itself not a phenomenon to be perceived, but a way of perceiving objects that would not be in space if we did not perceive them to be, is too conceptual. A more adequate version would be: what we call *space* is a way of *behaving* with objects that *presumes* space. Or, space is a presumption we must accept in order to live with objects. This is compatible with what Nagarjuna from his buddhist monastery in India argued: simply that space is a verbal convenience; it has no inherent nature so how could it exist?

What of "unimpedingness" as a suggestive description? Space as what does not impede, a tempting thought. It makes good sense of the way we maneuver through the everyday maze. The notion space can be eased out of our thinking by taking the everyday maze as a finely spun interweave of functions, as a reciprocal interpenetration of one's habits and the properties and behavior of extended things. If an axe of a certain length is brought down between a pair of legs distanced appropriately from the block of wood to be cut and swung by a back and pair of arms of the right length, the block of wood will be split or soundly struck. When city folk take their first turn at the woodpile, with little success, it is clear how much learned habit is needed to bring our behavior into functional congruence with axe and wood. A serving table in the kitchen, positioned so that with one or two steps, both hands loaded, one opens the swinging doors to the dining room with elbows, is a fine example of calculated extendedness. A staircase takes one from one floor to the next in the dark if one's legs know the height and number of steps. And we push and pull and turn knobs and buttons and levers when we drive a car—and with no sense of space whatsoever.

It is true we *talk* space at times, but usually as an ellipsis. We say a house is "spacious" if the rooms are of large dimension and promise some freedom of movement. We say there is no space for a piano in a room, when we mean the distances between the other objects will not accept the dimensions of the piano. Is space a way of sensing ease of movement in a maze of objects of varying shape and size that do not everywhere touch each other¿ Space quietly providing the possibility of movement¿

Movement

So, movement and behavior have arrived to help out. Movement of course draws in the question of time, for movement is as much "in time" as it is "in space." The way we measure space by time is common and fascinating. "How far is the city from here¿" "Oh, a good three hours drive." And that is an adequate measurement of distance for everyday purposes. When astronomers talk of the distances between galaxies or between planets and stars on the Milky Way they revert to measurement by time: the speed of the movement of light. Movement, time, and space in one cluster of thoughts, and space remains in the background. Time and movement are inseparable, but space remains a puzzle. What does it add to the equation, except that it allows us to believe we understand how movement is possible.

But why talk with Galileo about heavenly bodies, as Kant did¿ That's philosophy of science, which presumes the reality of the very space that is vivially so illusive. So goodbye Galileo and Kant; and not even hello to relativity theory—curved space, point instants, space-time continuum, non-Euclidian space. And for that matter not to Euclidian space either. Geometry doesn't explore the nature of space. It constructs certain shapes—circles, triangles, squares, cubes—that not only presuppose space itself, but presuppose it as something mathematical and material. Just what has proved not to be so, though it is our common faith. Relativity theory is in the same limbo when faced with vivial questions. Its theories depend upon an implicit understanding of spatialness—nowhere justified—for their intelligibility. Space is not their concern and continues to ghost in the background as presumption. The theories themselves, whatever their importance for theoretical physics and space warfare, do not further the exploration of lived space and its worth for the vivial sense of things.

Space as a physical medium, as quantitative, as objective, as the possibility of solid bodies moving and accelerating at calculable speeds has proved to be a dry well. The many ways behavior interweaves with extended objects have given some solid meaning to our uses of the word space, without space declaring itself in its own right. Can space do that? *Is* there space in our everyday understanding of it? So far, no sign of it.

Home of Human Worth

But does more not happen in and through the space that has not been discovered in the everyday than the movement of lifeless bodies? What about *expressive* body movement? What of the child throwing a temper tantrum? The child is dancing a dance of helpless rage. His or her legs and arms and body are moving "in space"—as much as Kepler's rolling balls were. But who attends to the speed and acceleration of these movements? Their significance for the child's inner life speaks to us, and they demand an understanding response. What of the political or religious orator who points his finger, now up, now down, or threshes his arms about? No one watching and listening believes he or she is merely observing a moving body; the observer feels the impact of a passionately, or apparently passionately, held belief. What is indeed body movement, becomes, in a human setting, its own kind of oratory. This is hardly a secret, but what fascinates is the way a movement "in space", as we commonly say, becomes a political or religious statement.

Of course, that it can be so is the basis for human and all animal societies. Body carriage speaks inarguably of the inner state of a being. We read dejection, contrition, buoyancy, contempt, sympathy in the posture and gestures of humans and even some animals. A raised eyebrow, a downward twist of the mouth, a smile are said to be movements "in space," too, and as such could probably be recorded in a graph. But, at the same time and inseparably, they express opinion or attitude—and that is the mystery. How does a significance we can't describe in terms of movement in space come to depend on what we commonly call "movement in space" for its manifestation? How do the two come together? If they are two. What actors can achieve on stage before they have said a word is at the heart of theater. Hamlet's initial wordless languor on the fringe of the court prepares us for his prevaricating speeches; and Shakespeare's Kings say more by their majestic bearing than by their often ornate speeches.

The "space" between people teems with ideas, emotions, intentions, innuendoes, flying as swiftly as light and sound back and forth and around. Human space is not empty! And how differently different ages fill it or don't fill it. Our hygenic, mathematically docile, empty space is unique. It allows our science to feel at home throughout the universe; and it grounds Western technologies. Semitic religions see space as the historical stage on which their god watches over his peoples. And space in the Sanskcrit Upanishads, being fine matter, could be the warp and woof on which Truth was woven. "Ignorant people," our scientists would say. "How much we have lost," I would reply.

Empty space is difficult to find politically, socially, or personally. Every nation has its own quality of space. The entire surround talks to one without interruption or words of the culture one is in. You can feel when you're in French space, or English, or American. Canada, some say, *is* space. And "north" and "south" are cultural spaces, without boundaries. Family space is charged with intimacies of half-told, half-guessed secrets, half-expressed and half-suppressed animosities, and so many—though fewer than supposed—common memories. Odd how space, which could not show itself among solid objects, is becoming the matrix of the world of feelings and ideas.

And doesn't social space overlap with person space? A French shrug is as personal as it is French. An American handshake is as personal as it is American. And the Canadian "eh?" is part of the person who says it. The interweave defies analysis. It is like an invisible nimbus, enlivening the space around a person with values and presumptions, mostly unaware, that are themselves anything but spatial—in our everyday sense.

Realists will say this is the height of improper metaphor. After all there is nothing to all this except normal sense perception; space problems can be ignored. Of course they can be, if one's interest is theory of sense perception. But for vivial exploration it is how we live our perceptions that counts, for that is where life sense is found. The "what does it matter" of the French shrug is not only a perception in the mind, it's taken as a body movement. Else, how read it correctly? Person space seems to tell the same story. It is commonly reported that Eastern peoples live in a larger private space than Westerners do. Certainly it is so that you can startle an Indian into withdrawal by advancing on him or her with outstretched North American hand. We're not usually startled until someone thrusts his face or body within a foot or two of our own.

And space is as individual as faces. One does not need auras to sense an envelope of space around a person into which he or she exudes their temperament or mood. And more. Each individual lives in his or her own world of space. Someone who lives with snowmobiles and four-wheel-drive trucks in winter is certainly in a different surround than someone who moves on skis. Though both move through the same woods. The one woods is full of noise and exhaust smells; the other is full of silence and the smell of body heat—and snow. We commonly say such two persons live in different worlds. And so they do. But to say each lives in a different spatial surround is more interesting, especially for an exploration of space. It tells us that character traits, habits of mind, interests—all nonspatial and invisible—can reach out into the world of supposedly spatial objects and bind them together into a stable vivial enclave reflecting back through "space" those same nonspatial interests and habits of mind. If that isn't a mystery! A spatial surround filled with the invisible traits of oneself. Fear of enclosed spaces makes the space itself frightening; and so does fear of not being enclosed. the openness frightens. Not withstanding all the theories of subject-object perception.

But person space is the most difficult of all space explorations. Something more accessible would make the same point more simply, like the movements of the performing dancer. As the art of pure movement, dancing speaks wordlessly of feelings and ideas that are themselves not spatial. Modern dance, ballet, Middle East female solo dancing, Indian storytelling dancing are, in this respect, no different. It seems that the movements are talking to us and yet are "in space"—if anything is. Debussy's faun moves his body, arms, and legs in ways that could be traced on a spatial graph; but their dreamy, smoldering significance could not be. This is so obvious; what is the point? For one thing, this is not semiotics: the faun's movements are not "signals" that "communicate" his feelings to an audience. A dancer's movements are related to their significance more closely than that. Signals can be coded in a system, indeed they're not signals until they are; and their significance is arbitrarily assigned to them. In dance, what the movement says is inseparable from the movement itself. There is no coded signal. The seductive grace of the faun's undulations is experienced as one phenomenon, spontaneous and unrepeatable. The two may be separated in concept—as now—but not in the experience. And so the question, how do we live space? returns in a less naive, and more difficult, form.

What can solid bodies not in motion—sculpture, architecture, painting—tell us that might help?

The Jama Masjid Mosque in Delhi and the Blue Mosque in Istanbul are objects "extended in space", no doubt. But as one lives them, object and space are no longer two. The Delhi mosque, open to the sky, its worn brick and flagstone shaping a "space" that reaches up to the greatness of Allah. The Istanbul mosque, wholly enclosed, its dark blue dome and curved walls rich with stone flowers of the most intense colors sanctify human passion. These are not merely extended stationary objects, but open and orbed "space" speaking the language of religious submission. And that Buddhist temple in Burma. It was in Mandalay. Mothers and fathers bringing their children into the round stone temple and crumbling a few flowers into the lap of the seated Buddha. It was like a family shrine, its "space" evoking humble devotion. The temple in "space" and the "space" in the temple were inseparable from each other and from the Buddha's great peace. Neither temple nor "space" were any longer spatial—unless peace itself can be!

Paintings are invasive. Tom Thompson and Emily Carr. What is that lurch they cause inside us? It's familiar; but now, hunting down the ghost of space, it's talking more clearly. Why do their trees come to mind as important? With Tom Thompson's indomitable pine tree on the rocky shore of a northern lake or Emily Carr's abandoned but undismayed fir tree in the wasteland of a logged-over rain forest, does the lurch have to do with suddenly seeing that trees are not measurable objects, standing lifeless in "space"? In their tree paintings, "space" seems to be taken up into the substance of the trees themselves; "space" becomes what allows the trees to stand forth, to become what they are, and to tell us that.

The laws of perspective may be as objective as the speed of

light, but those two trees are no longer "in space". Emily Carr's machine slaughter of a clear-cut forest allows the one spindly fir tree, ignored as worthless, quite alone between earth and heaven, to come to life as struggling to lift its indomitable head up to the light. That tree, "scorned as timber, beloved of the sky," is no longer a mere object "in space", but is alive in a field of human values. What our everyday tells us is space becomes somehow transformed, as if it had been waiting for the chance to become the potential of Carr's indomitability. Yes. But what becomes of "space"? What becomes of "objects"?

So that's where my exploration is heading. It's not quite proper. Most people will concede that the transformation of space into a field of human values may, as metaphor, hold for poetry, painting, sculpture, architecture, and theater, but not for everyday reality as it is before artists transform it: in the everyday we experience space as it is. Well, not all our beliefs hold true. What if *all* human behavior is its own kind of artistry; and *all* objects "in space" can carry human values?

In the presence of a 100 foot maple tree there is an easy majesty; and a great spruce is imperturbably solemn and wise; and an aged oak has a timeless strength no human can match. What are we doing when we say that majesty, solemnity, strength are qualities of the trees, even though the qualities themselves, we commonly believe, exist only in human minds? Are they qualities of the tree as its height and diameter are, or its distinctive wood? Obviously not, but they are not merely subjective either. Of course all human attribution, even dimensions and shape, gathers objects into the human world; but for now the question concerns nonphysical attributes. Whether it is trees or lakes, rocks, or clouds, the qualities we commonly attribute to them—threatening, serene, ageless, and so on—are unthinkable apart from human experience and are obviously not formations "in space". It is so. But these human attributions need spatial objects. Somehow they ride on their very bodies. They are not labels pasted capriciously or poetically on the objects of nature. Some things *are* threatening, some serene, some ageless. Things must be able to accept our experiences of their natures, or we couldn't consistently live with them—short of madness. A pail of water cannot be inviolably serene, as a lake or calm ocean naturally is; that much is clear. It seems that humanly qualified objects are neither "in" the mind nor "in space". They exist in the symbiosis of the two. They are both inner and outer and yet neither exclusively. Each is discovered as the other retires. Which, of course, defies conceptual analysis.

Is this the "pathetic fallacy" that Ruskin and the critics of his day so decried: the fallacy of attributing purely subjective states to purely inanimate objects? It most certainly is not. It is the "pathetic fallacy" that can be seen as pathetic in its fallaciousness. Sundering the world into objective and subjective is just what vivial exploring finds a root error. Nor does the metaphoric compromise see the problem squarely. There is more vivial sense in seeing subjective and objective as balancing emphases of one experience. Nothing can be perfectly and merely object or perfectly and merely subject, the one apart from the other. That would be to canonize everyday belief. "Objective" and "subjective" have become very questionable terms.

Inner and outer proved to be ready ideas for many everyday purposes, though neither can be real in itself. Each loses its independence in experience. And "space" has turned out to be a primordial instance of the symbiosis of inner and outer. Someone who insists that a tree is merely an object in space, merely outer, pulls the very guts out of our experience of its majesty and solemnity. It is a fallacy, truly pathetic, to hold that such qualities belong only to my mind, not to the tree. At one stroke this kills the worth of the tree and the worth of my own mind. The tree becomes a stick of wood, and my mind a madhouse of floating feelings. That makes no vivial sense. The world would have no intrinsic value except for buying and selling. And experience of the world would be robbed of any relevance to one's sense of the worth of things.

And of course we do more than "see" the world: we hear it, if possible more unceasingly. What of the movement of air in space that becomes sound for us? Well, apart from theories of perception, which serve a different purpose, sound is naively lived as belonging to the outer world just as plainly as a seen object is. And it is equally measurable and hence objective; and equally, though differently, spatial, as we can locate its source in space and describe the spatial events that make it. Yet sounds are even more trenchantly non-spatial than seen objects. They cut into feelings more immediately and more deeply than visual objects do. That is as true of the human voice in anger or tenderness as of the first bird song in spring. But when sound is composed to give voice to human experience below the verbal threshold and then reaches one through musical instruments, we don't distinguish the "sounds" heard through the ear from the emotions they arouse. Except for technical purposes. The "sound" of violin or piano or voice or orchestra, whatever the musical complexities, *is* "rousing" or "lilting", "demonic" or "soothing". The measurable sound is one with the experience. So perfectly we seldom call the contradiction to mind.

Mask of the Boundless

It is becoming inescapable: "space", measurable and objective and indispensable in our everyday world, is, nonetheless, not a reality but a way of covering over the depth and worth both of the world and ourselves. The vigor of the tree, the grace of the dancer, the vitality of the painting, the emotional power of music, the life-shaping forms of architecture are not the sole property of the "outer" objects and no more the sole property of an "inner" state. The two are not two in experience. The life qualities of natural and art objects have a way of being for which we have no name. A strange line of thought—with no end in sight. This much is now certain: to treat outer objects either as possessing nothing but their spatial properties—pathetic fallacy; or as naturally possessing all qualities we give them in the everyday—guilty look, lilting sound, elegant gesture—is to fail to grasp the symbiosis of inner and outer. It's becoming clear that a sense of spaciousness permeates our experience in a way that stands the pathetic fallacy on its head, though I'm not sure how to grasp it.

Here comes a thought that hasn't surfaced into words yet. Can I say objects in our everyday world are not *in* space, but reveal an *openness* to us? If we care to attend. This openness cannot be a quality of objects as their bodily properties are. Is it that objects have their shapes, stand out as what they are, against a background of the *absence* of physical space. Must our naive, everyday notion of physical space transparence into its own absence if we are to experience objects as arrayed each for itself around us? Is "openness" the possibility of solid bodies having any shape at all? And must it be "empty", that is, not there, if it is to have this possibility?

If this is so then our everyday space turns out not to be an attribute of the external world. That is still a contradiction, but indefeasible. We use a vague notion of quantitative space pervasively in our everyday doings. But that space, on being interrogated as to what it might be, withdraws—how else to put it—behind the external order of objects that it, itself, in its new guise of openness, makes possible. The everyday notion of space marks a boundary of attribution. We believe the vibration of a violin string is in space, but not the sweetness of its sound. We believe the spire of a cathedral is in space, but not its impregnable serenity. Our everyday notion of space, either as extendedness itself or as the element in which bodies are extended, excludes the range of attributes that carry all human worth. The spatial order of the everyday, thus abstracted, would make a ghost wasteland, interesting only to physical science. The irrepressible strength of trees, the grace of dance, the fine significance of facial gestures, would be denied a home in that wasteland because they refuse to be conceived as spatial.

This is a crux. Space as physical and extended is not a real element in our lived world. It is real only as a necessary illusion, interwoven with other natural beliefs to make a livable everyday—and mathematical science. Still, the illusion is so natural that it is useful to continue to speak of "everyday space", but only in this sense. So, though there is a mystery in the way non-spatial values can live happily in "everyday space", there is nothing objectionable in saying that they do. And it avoids both a bifurcated world—subjective and objective—and two worlds—perceptual and transcendental. The lived world is not composed of valueless solid objects in real space and immaterial feelings and ideas in my mind. Serenity can come to us from calm waters, sympathy from a smile, mercilesssness from tornadoes and electric storms. That much is now clear. But *how* are the two related? That's the rub. It is not just an empirical association, though most would argue that it is. Rather, value attributes are not merely the guests of "spatial objects," but—and this is the paradox—they are themselves, in some sense, naturally spatial, though not in the everyday sense. They come to us as spread out—in an openness that is a "space" that is not there. The indomitability of Emily Carr's and Tom Thompson's trees is not an abstraction, a concept, a name superimposed on them arbitrarily. It is borne by the upthrusting shape of the trees in the surrounding openness. By what else? The grace of the dancer makes no sense as an attribute of a mere moving body. Yet it is undeniably, and indefinably, spread out, spatial. It is a spread-out grace borne by body movement in a "space" that can be experienced only as a transformation of everyday space. Realized in its absence one must say. It is this presence in absence that allows body movement to have shape and worth; that is, to be what it is. So it is with objects. The serenity of water is spread through its entire body. The spirit of temples and cathedrals pervades them without favoritism of aspect or locus.

Are there then two spaces? No. One is mystery enough. One could oppose the everyday space of solid bodies to an unthinkable second space that is absent even as it seems present. But that's not how we live it. We can make only a distinction between, not a disjunction of, our everyday notion of space and the reality of spatial objects bearing the values we discover in them. This much we can hold on to: value attributes, seemingly incorporeal, and the solid objects of our everyday are not from two worlds. They are like broken fragments of one world that comes into being for us when they find each other.

How understand the two, if they are two, as one? How understand the one if it were not two? To both questions the answer is: we can't. A dualism of body and spirit, mind and matter, perception and thought makes understanding impossible. It perpetuates an ancient Greek and Christian cleavage of the human being that cannot serve us well today. And it burdens us with the crippling pathetic fallacy of inner and outer. The idealist offers us a transcendental realm and is complacent. But idealism throws a frustrating blanket of moral values over the stubborn character of solid objects and suffocates their integrity. It denies the mystery of twoness in one. And it is blind to the essential quality of human experience. Some contemporaries would say the world is torn from the inner life of the person in self-destruction; that the person turns itself inside out, and finds itself again in the way of the world. Good. But there is more to the world than the anguish of persons, though at times it seems not much more. How do full honor to this world we live in that pretends to be measurably spatial but is not, a world that becomes a human world only by grace of the boundless possibility of human values arriving in it like guests from nowhere? Values that are at home here as if they belonged to solid objects. Where does that leave the everyday world? What does it leave us of space? Can we any longer believe that we know what space is? No, for sure. Language refuses to serve that purpose.

Again the conundrum: human values are not spatial, yet come to meet us only as oned with objects we take to be spatial, and without which they would not be our food and drink, but remain floating fantasies.

It's odd to be saying things like that, but it is the plain outcome of a little exploration. What can be said at this point but that "space", in which our everyday world appears to be displayed, is a transparent stage set for something that is not everyday "space". Was what the Upanishads were trying to say perhaps something like this? They could urge the revering of space because space was not empty, not isolated in a world of its own but the natural element and framework on which cosmic Truth could be woven "like warp and woof".

Well, enough of space for now.

What has become clear so far? The experiences that we name "grace", "grandeur", "serenity", "evil", are not capable of arising for us in any other way than through our belief in a world of solid objects, including the human body, in "space". Such experiences are unable to become present for us except through the clumsy language and theater that is our everyday world. They, for whatever reason—Chuang Tzu liked to say "If the great ones do not know the reason, why should I?"—must pretend to be at home in a world of solid objects if they are even to whisper their presence to us. We humans could not discover them otherwise. Thinking this way, at least life is lived in a cosmos, one meaningful world. A human can move from the rough gobs of everyday objects to the source of their worth, without belittling or denying either and without denying any part of himself or herself. The senses and spirit are not two. As we can listen to a beginner stumble through a well-known melody and *hear* the melody in the false notes.

So, what is space? This is no longer a proper question. Everyday "space" has become certainly less than we take it to be, and as certainly more than nothing: a kind of cipher, lacking intelligible character. But it is a word that has led out into the open, boundless depth of our lived world. What gave itself to be measurable, finite spreadoutness, in and between solid objects, was from the beginning a lure, a fumbling attempt of things and humans to disclose the rich openness of the human world. Feet and inches the mask of the boundless! This isn't the crude "infinity" of boundless "space", but the boundless range of human experience.

Space has become an elemental test of the symbiosis of inner and outer. When "space" becomes the home of human values echoing back from regions that are not spatial but more the freedom of the unbounded, then inner and outer cease to be two and the world becomes one. So it will seem.

A final irony. Space is inexpungable so long as one, in the busyness of the everyday, brackets out the vivial worth of things. It is the most obvious, most pervasive, least questionable element in the reality of the everyday. But it is not there. What does this do to the claim of the everyday world to be *the* reality? How does something that is wholly unintelligible sustain itself forever in our natural world? By magic? But that is a further question.

Space, you child of the obvious, where are you leading me?

TIME

Clocks and Calendars

Well, "space" left a deep gash in our common faith that whatever we must take to be real in order to live as we do is real as we take it to be. As a rock bottom feature of reality, space evanesced. Leaving the realist indignant at my superficial comments. And me awe-struck at the reality of the imperceptible.

But space has a twin from which it is seldom parted: time. Time is even more importunately given in its reality, both for the everyday and for science, than is space. If that is possible. Time is our assurance of an objective world, even though we don't perceive it, as we mistakenly believe we perceive space. It is the "passage of time", as we put it, that we believe we experience. And the reality of that is guaranteed by the precision and universality of the units by which we measure the passing of time. A second is a second from the South Pole to the North Pole. So with minutes and hours and days and months and years. What could be more rock solid? What else could make a framework for ensuring coherent social behavior and for executing precision tasks? For measuring the duration of natural processes and the movements of our sun and moon and all astronomical bodies? And for understanding human and prehuman history? We can't conceive of reality apart from time.

So we believe. But our time units are more social conventions than we commonly bother to remember. A day hardly unrolls in twenty-four fixed periods except where a society has decided so to measure it. And no society except our own has. That Greeks and Romans, and Babylonians and the ancient Chinese and Indians, knew nothing of the sixty-minute "hour", preferring to live their day in ten longer periods, or in half a dozen "watches", or simply by the position of the sun and moon, raises the question of the reality of our everyday "time". The movements of earth and moon with respect to the sun haven't changed. In the days of Rome one rotation of the earth would have taken approximately twenty-four of our hours, as it does now, and would today take approximately ten of the units used by the romans. In neither case, the astronomers tell us, would the measurement be precise. But that is irrelevant. It's the difference between the diurnal rotation and the time units by which we measure it, that *is* relevant. And striking. The same with seconds and minutes. That they are of relatively recent devising in the West, however precisely—cesium atoms or vibrating rods—we define what they are to mean, reminds us that they are a human convention.

The bizarre character of our "time" units makes the point beautifully. They are a grabbag from history. Seconds, minutes, and hours are borrowed from geometry and the compass. Our "day" is twenty-four "hours" measured from the midpoint of darkness; others have measured their day from one sundown to the next. Our "week" is of Hebrew origin, carried wherever Christianity went. And unique, I believe. Other civilizations clustered their days in bundles of ten, or in lunar fortnights, or counted them in relation to fixed festivals. That the moon takes roughly twenty-nine and a half days to complete a waxing and waning has been known to all classical civilizations. But we're alone in numbering the days of each month consecutively from number 1. That's straightforward. Trouble comes in working the extra half day into the sequence of months. Some round off each month at thirty days and keep the left-over five or six days dangling at the end of the year without any number. We adopted the wishes of the Christian church and scattered the half days through the year—seven months of thirty-one days, four of thirty, one of twenty-eight—and named each month from ancient mythologies.

And so many ingenious ways to marry up the twenty-nine and a half days of the moon cycle with the three hundred and sixty-five and one-quarter days of the earth's orbit. It makes the point just to think of them. What of continuing the cycle of thirty-day months unbroken into the new year so that the five extra days push the beginning of the new year ahead by five days each and every year? Muslims do. Simple. But for our round of festivals bewildering. Every thirty years or so New Year and Christmas would fall in mid-summer, and we would be planting our crops at harvest time! How our *lived* year differs according to the "time" units we experience it in!

The point is becoming pretty clear. But there are still other fascinating peculiarities we live with as natural. What of the number of our calendar year? We are *living*, with every letter or check we write, with every calculation of our own age, as if it is a fact of nature that this year is number 1993. And from that we think ahead to the state of the world at the "end of the century". Or backward to grasp our historical evolution from the years before Christ through the fall of Rome in 410 A.D., the discovery of America in 1492, the Renaissance in the fifteenth and sixteenth centuries, the emergence of the modern West in the eighteenth and nineteenth centuries. All "time" is divided into the ages before Christ and the centuries after his birth.

We live with our own numbers shaping all time for us, even though, when we stop to think, we remember that not all peoples live their past in our numbered units. If this year were really 1993 A.D., how could Buddhists be living in the year 2537 B.E.? And Muslims in 1414 A.H.? The numbers we live with give the years a quality all their own. We speak of the "thirties" or the "sixties" and they bring so much of our past to life. The Great Depression and the beginning of the Second World War could not happen in the "twenties" or "fifties." That would fracture our reality. Don't we grasp ourselves as from the year of our birth? Could a 50-year old Westerner recognize himself or herself as born in 2487 or 1364? And yet it would be no less true, and no more arbitrary, than 1943. This is childishly obvious, yet how seldom we feel the strain it puts on our sense of time?

Then there's the most pervasive and vivially decisive of the tricks we play with time: living by clocks and watches! Their numbers make time so real, we live time through them. "What *is* the time?" The time *is* 11 P.M." That "is" tricks us. In Newfoundland the time is 1 A.M. of the next day; in Delhi they're already having lunch—tomorrow; but in Hawaii they're just sitting down to supper, today. How can we think the "is" of clock time? Time zones don't explain away the lived quality of the numbers on our watch—their reality. If there are twenty-four time zones, are there twenty-four different, but equally real, "times"? Absurd. But still there is the question, "What is the real time?" It is a real question, but one without a meaningful answer.

"What day of the week *is* it?" Same trick. Here it *is* Saturday. But in half the world it *is* Sunday, so far as our names for the days are used. Just fifty miles down the road it is midnight and Sunday is beginning. Again the name of day is not the naming of a reality, but an essential part of the social world we live in. "Saturday" means no school, no office; "Sunday" means church or visits or picnics; "Monday" means the grindstone of a new week. And that is the essential function of time conventions: they shape our days and weeks for us. "7 A.M." says get up; "12 noon" says lunch break; "11 P.M." says bedtime. And the everlasting *quantity* of time available for accomplishing our tasks, as ticked into our ear and twitched into our eye by our watches, must insinuate a quantitative quality into our sense of life itself.

Clock time is the structure of the thick weave of habits we clothe ourselves in. We live in a habitat of clock time as we do in one of measured space, and no less does Western science. One could say that mathematical space and time have created an unnatural world for humans to live in. But time as social convention or scientific postulate is not the time a vivial exploration is seeking. We pervasively, if unawarely, live our routines, work, chores, not only as so much clock time, but as hateful, enjoyable, boring, creative. Whether gardening, selling, washing dishes, the task itself brings a quality to the experience and a sense of its duration. Duration is not a quantity; it is short or long, swift or dragging, but always lived more as a quality—unlike clock intervals. The hour of waiting for an important decision can be as half a day, or an eternity. The hour spent writing a poem can be one round drop of time.

What is this duration? It is not lived in quantities. Is it the way we experience time? Is it merely subjective? That is something no one has ever been able to make clear to me—not Augustine, nor Kierkegaard, nor Heidegger, nor the Indians, nor the Taoists. In any case it is firm: there is no excuse for confusing a complex of time units with time itself. That is negative, but it's a start. And what clever person can separate negative from positive?

So clocks and calendars are not very fertile sources for an exploration of time. They are mere masks thrown over time as we live it, concealing the ebb and flow of lived duration. All right. But then, what is duration if not the passage of time? Well, that's now the question. If our everyday time has evanesced, what remains? Presumably time, in some other conception. We can't live in an unmapped ocean. "Time" is a grand and mighty word and must hold grand and mighty secrets in its vastness.

Especially for us moderns and postmoderns in our naturalistic world. It has long since been decided for us that human life is rooted in temporal process, that all there is or can be unfolds in time. In a religious age, and for one who lives religiously in any age, humankind is rooted in the timeless. The ancient Taoists and Confucians, Buddhists, Hindus, and Christians would have been shocked, or amused, at our causal and temporal succession of all happenings as the one flat landscape of human life.

But today, in our complacent scientific wisdom and timorous religious faith, we have no assured way of passing through clock time and exploring what may lie behind it, without succumbing to idealism or narcissism. Thanks to the scientists for impelling us to search afresh for what they have assured us we can do without.

How to set about this? How begin what has no beginning? How probe for the invisible contours of a landscape that may, or may not, lie behind clock and calendar time? Of course, even without clocks and calendars we are still enfolded in a sinewy weave of time notions, which, in their turn, insinuate themselves into our behavior and demand the status of reality be conferred on them.

In the everyday pursuit of ambitions and desires, it seems we naturally, or have been taught to believe that we naturally understand all happenings in three phases. The decisive phase is the "present," when action becomes possible; so long as anticipated events are in the open field of planning and manipulation we say they are in the "future"; when they have been through the present and no longer can be influenced, we say they are in the "past". Behavior is understood to be the fitting of present acts into anticipated events drawing on experience from the past. There we have it! If we're not on our guard we'll believe we have captured time in its three phases, modes, or as some have it, "ecstasies" of past, present, and future.

But a sense of "not yet", "is", and "was" is endemic to human behavior—if given lesser or greater embrace in different societies. It is as close to us as reaching out for a drink, enjoying it, and setting down the empty cup or glass. Time in this sense is, with space, the most pervasively enabling presumption of our behavior. We would be adrift in limbo without it. It is the element in which our feelings and ideas live, like fish in water. How distance oneself from it far enough to explore it¿ To test future, present, past for their sense¿

Well, not by the realist question, "What are they¿" because they may not be whats, and to look for them as such might lead me unaware right past them. After all, time may be a ghost that speaks no human language. "How do we live what we call past, present, and future¿" is more promising. It will allow the exploration to begin right here and now and does not presume a theoretical answer. Just a probing into the experiences time words lead me to; no search for definable meanings. "Sense" is more important, being inseparable from ways of experiencing, from behavior. Sense, not meaning, is the natural worth of an idea. A vivial exploration cannot proceed on the legs of definitions.

Iz, Waz, To-Be, in the Now

Begin with what is closest. Where and how and when are we closest to the experience of moving with the flow of present, past, and future¿ The closest will be the least clear, but it should be the most fecund. Can we get any closer than we are when we say "now"¿ Aren't we standing in the very current of time when it moves through us in the "now"¿ And future "nows" stand in queue upstream, waiting to become the present "now". And each one passing through the present takes its place in the endless line of past "nows" lying lifeless downstream. Is that not our sense of "now"¿ It must have great pragmatic value to justify its universality.

But the disjunction of future, present, and past makes little vivial sense. Now is torn out of its lived context and made into an abstract entity identified as the present. This presumes an imaginary transverse sector of time forming the boundary between future and past. But if time flows incessantly then it will be flowing *during* the present! Or else we think of the present now as a mere metaphorical line drawn across the flow of nows. But that, apart from confusing space and time, violates the sense of important duration we experience as peculiar to the present.

Peculiar because of the happening of actions and events. Now is the only way time can strike home. Action lends its name to the actual. Future possibilities and past memories become the material for action only as they become actual. An act is evidence of the isness of an existent world even as it confers the status of reality on that world. Insofar as act is distinctive of now, now can be said to be our opening onto the world and the world's presence for us.

But an act is not a lightening flash from nowhere. It is clothed in purposes, calculations, decisions; and all these cannot be squeezed into a tight is. They reach forward into the nonexistent future. That tells me something new about now: the future is *in* the now, or the future "izes" in the now. We say goals are "in the future", but as intentions they are as present as the act itself. They are the substance of action. An act is what it is only when understood as the enactment of its purpose. The future, as intention, is as integral to now as the actual. The not-yet-existent is as actual as the existent. Bizarre. Yet it is so.

But action is not two-legged—present and future—else where would the substance of intentions come from? The content of what is foreseen as the to-be but is not yet must arise from what one has already experienced: from the past. Aided by the imagination. The present, as the strictly actual, could not of itself tell us anything about what might be. A feeble grasp of the past permits only a shallow grasp of the future. A sense of who I have been is integral to my understanding of who I am and might be in the future. Could one act awarely into the future, trust one's own promises or see through one's pretensions, if something of the past were not always with one as teacher? Could one be aware that there is a future if one had no past in the form of memory?

So now is not merely two-legged, it has a third stem. At first glance a synonym for the present, now seems more a magical interweave of future and past as well. It is not so much a moment *in* time as a capsule *of* time—if time means past, present, and future. No right to say that. I have no idea yet how to use the word time. Now, it seems, is not merely the present, but allows future and past to be present as well. Sounds contradictory. Well, how do we experience future and past?

What once was present is, for the present that is just "izing", past, embalmed in the dead "was"—yet as alive as all presence, and so, the "waz". Waz experiences are alive in the present as memories and, metamorphosed, become the substance of the future. What was is withdrawn from our will as Nietzsche pointed out. Yet as the izing waz it influences our intentions, providing the substance of our picture of what might be. What was also helps constitute the present through our common belief that what was causally generates consequences in the present and allows us to understand some of our izing feelings and intentions. The heart and backbone of the present is the sense of continuous life from what was to what is. We take ourselves as shaped and empowered by the unbroken flow of sense from the past.

The future, what is to-be but not yet is, seems to be bonded to the present by some form of interest—appetitive compulsion, curiosity, ambition, fear, whatever may become the substance of action. Differently than waz is. Waz is the base of the actual, given in its own right, only through unaware falsification dependent on the iz. To-be is more dependent on the iz, being almost one with it. Its vitality, unlike that of waz, is not its own. Yet, what is pictured as to-be lets life flow into the present and rescues it from being a lifeless photograph of existing facts. The foreseen to-be shapes behavior, most often as the continuous substance of actual intentions. How an absent what-is-not-yet can be the substance of what is, is a wondrous riddle and the very nature of to-be. Alter the to-be and you alter the present. As anyone knows who has observed how altered career plans generate altered habits and interests in the present.

Heidegger and Husserl would not share my emphasis. Husserl's fascination with the intricacies of memory retention leaves the future dangling, unlived. Heidegger's primacy of the future allows him to discover the meaning of human existence in possible stances toward it and allows the past to fade in significance. Were they of two different ages?

Seen my way, to-be and waz subtend from the izing present even as they provide its substance. They are so much one with it in the living now that we could say now is not a moment *in* the flow of time, squeezed between one moment before and another after, but is the elemental experience *of*—time? Will it help to say now is the vehicle of time? But what is the metaphor worth? Is there not more worth in the thought that now is the vehicle of life, as what allows a continuous self-understanding? If it were only that simple. If only now were more honest. Waz is only what is available to us in memory of the infinitely complicated experiences that once ized, so the to-be that lends meaning to our acts is a distorted picture fed by memories of but a small portion of our lived experiences. Now is not a vessel capturing the disinterested flow of an obligingly honest self-understanding.

Thanks to Nietzsche for reminding us that our now is more a whirlpool of ignorance and self-deception than a light-filled intelligence. Now is the tireless fountain of distortions generated by the conceit and cowardice that humans acknowledge themselves heir to. In the now both what was and the to-be are bent to the needs of the iz—those of action in a given reality, including inner action in an inner reality. It is as though now was confined within two great contoured mirrors, both distorting: the one, memory, reflecting only as much of what was as the iz can bring itself to accept; the other, foresight, picking up the crippled images from the mirror of waz and further contorting them before passing them back to the iz as what is to-be.

But mirrors don't generate the images they reflect, nor are images blown in from the passing wind of momentary situations. What gives them their vitality? For a sharp memory or fear of a future event have the full kick of the present. What can it be but the iz? What izes, from the clearest memories and anticipations to unworded thought pulsions and diffuse feelings, must arise from the brooding ground deep beneath our everyday consciousness. Every pulsion that izes must bubble up from somewhere spontaneously, in the sense of not being willed. *That* consciousness izes, clearly owes nothing to the waz or the to-be, as these have their life only as subtended from iz. To offer explanations for the magic of izing, the miracle of actual awareness, would be to assume it was less than spontaneous. Which it isn't. Now is more than two mirrors; iz gives life and substance to the images they reflect. And it is the human lot to be unable to generate the waz and the to-be except as what lies in the interest of the actual.

Am I losing sight of time? Thinking of past, present, and future as waz, iz, and to-be strips them of the character of time as ineluctable succession: first future, then present, and then past. Does "now" obscure time? Well. I'm not exploring for a definition of time. I'm exploring our ways of experiencing time, what its sense is for us. But sense is inseparable from behavior—inner valuing as well as outer actions. So the question becomes, what range of *experience* does each of waz, iz, and to-be point to? Even if the pointing is only rarely explicit. What is not yet, but is to-be—graduation, marriage, the end of the century—is most often an interim terminal in our plans around which we fit detailed actions required to realize them or that will follow upon their being realized. The to-be is a behaviorally functional field subtended from the iz. "Future" seems to be a superfluous word. People of a compulsive, activist nature live in the to-be, for the most part unawarely. Their future goals are their present reality and vice versa. Obstacles, danger, or trenchant promise at times awaken a sense of the distance of such goals from the actual, of how much living—not time—lies between. And this can arouse fear or hope or greed so sharply that the sense of behavioral distance becomes explicit as the difference of the nonactual to-be from the actual is, and this evokes the sense we are conditioned to think of as the "future". That we are powerless in face of the great structure of things—the end of the world, death—also marks off the to-be. But this in no way presents itself as time.

Our experience of the present is no less inconclusive. Sometimes we live the becoming existent of what was to-be—graduation, the moment at the altar. Then we can be startled into awareness that what is, izes right here as present reality. Immediate perception and reality are two faces of one experience. What we mean by the present is recognizable most surely by the overwhelming sense of reality izing right *here* where one is behaving; and in this it marks itself off from the more distant *there* of the to-be. Space again. But this must be quite rare. In the everyday both the to-be and the iz function perfectly without any help from our awareness of them. In all this neither to-be nor iz need the addition of the notion time—future or present—to be what they are experienced as.

Is it just because I am old that at times the past is the weightiest of the triad, feeding more into wisdom and self-understanding than future and present do? The izing moment vanishes into the depths of the past more swiftly, more bafflingly than an oil lamp into the magician's smoke. Where did the last heartbeat go to? Not Husserl's "retention" of it, but the reality of it. What was may surface again as the waz, distant, even unreal. Yet the power of the past never lets us go. It is the untouchable, immutable, ancient, abiding waz, the history of peoples and civilizations and persons. There is something awesome in the presence of a "dead" past that has infinitely more lasting life in it than present or future have. That awe tells me the past is present, that what was is izing—a more haunting experience than present or future. The past is like a monstrous maw swallowing all the little dead realities that iz, and permitting thereafter mere glimpses of them through its ancient teeth, glimpses we call memories. As the future is the natural habitat of the young and the enterprising, so all that can waz is most present for our contemplative moods and years.

Has this turned up anything more about present, past, and future? Some, not too much. Taken singly each shows no need for the notion of time, but when interfused in now a sense of something more than behavioral functions ghosts about in the background making now possible. But it remains unnamed. Many produce the word "temporality" out of the hat. Heidegger defines time as the happening of temporality, but this does not further a vivial exploration.

So far time has not been awaiting discovery in the streets of past, present, and future, nor at the Place du Now.

Behavior and Iz, Waz, To-Be

Puzzling enough for a pause. And a recollection from abroad. Time has not always been the dominant horizon of human behavior and sense as it has been for Greek-Europeans. And most certainly it has not everywhere been the future-thrusting juggernaut of natural process and evolution most Europeans and Americans accept today. It's not that the processes of nature and their ubiquitous mortality are not the elemental experience of humans everywhere. It is that these have not everywhere and always been understood and lived primarily as phenomena of time.

The Sanskrit Upanishads tell much about this. Their way of centering on the problem of the unchanging in a world that seems to show nothing but change is not a concern with time, in our sense. Uddalaka's analogy of the goldsmith refashioning a gold bracelet into a gold necklace using the identical piece of gold has a serene clarity. The universal spiritual substance—*Brahman*—is pure gold in its malleability and unique worth. Yajnavalkya's idealistic emphasis on the presence of unchangeable spirit—*Brahman*—in the self-awareness of every mortal subject is a different philosophy, but no less indifferent to our problem of time.

The Buddhist obsession with the moment-by-moment perishing of all things, both substantial outer things and inner states of consciousness, though different from the Upanishads, is an equally powerful reminder that the perishability of all things can be the center of a vivial thinking without our problem of time dictating the meaning of the question. Buddha makes the point simply. After his enlightenment he said only, "The imperishable, the deathless, has been attained". Not the timeless.

It can't be without some importance that classical Indian thought did not hold time to be the medium that defines how human life and all things must unfold—as we do. Perhaps for most it is the perishing of someone in the family that first bursts into the experience of the perishability of things, of death. It opens up a hollow space in one's world: one who had been there is now gone. This is not the mere sudden absence of a person or thing, it is that what once existed now does not. It's the loss that strikes home, the perishing. It seems to be this irremediable, implacable wasness of a person that arouses a sense of the difference between is and was—a truly vivial discovery. Things perish, too. The crudely leveled site of the ancestral farmhouse, now tractor seeded by a large landowner, can also leave a void in one's world. The was is discovered, not explicitly as a mode of time, but more as a mode of being: perishableness. To refer to humans as mortal is not to see them as beings of time, but of death. The existent is, by definition, immune to perishing. But who hasn't found out that the actual is the forecourt of the goneness of what was?

Was as what has perished makes sense, but what about the

to-be? Don't plans, goals, hopes—the commonest citizens of the to-be—perish as often and as readily as they come to be, leaving us forlorn in their goneness? When dreams melt and desires are frustrated, that is also a perishing. Hopes and dreams iz as all things do. But to-be is no less the womb of birth. What is actual and perishes must arise, and where can it arise except from the unborn, the to-be? Just to watch dead leaves in the forest making the birthing spot for next year's seeds is enough to awaken the thought of a cycle from birth through existence to death—and on to new birth. Not to mention caterpillars and butterflies! And this cycle holds for ideas in the mind and feelings in the heart, each dying in its successor, even as it gives birth to it. It is as true of empires as it is of families. This is the cycle, not just of birth and death, but, as Buddhists and Vedantists remind us, of rebirth.

The religious impact of this idea is history. But it is a striking reminder that Western "time" has not been the horizon of vivial sense everywhere. And need not be accepted by ourselves—in spite of prestigious advocacy. Buddhist *samsara*—the cycle of life forces from birth to death to birth—is less a stream of time flowing from future through present to past than a cycle of the perishable renewing itself. This seems to be their primordial way of making sense of human life. Time divisions and time language are of secondary concern, and why not? They feel they have their home in a realm that is impervious to destruction: *nirvāṇa*. For the Taoist it is the *Tao*; for Vedantists, oneness with unchanging *Brahman*. They would find our temporality moving on us from the future a singular stance.

This recollection throws the dominance of time in our lives into sharp relief. Our understanding of time, placed beside other cultures and philosophies, is historical, naturalistic, futuristic, nihilistic. As heaven recedes, human life is abandoned to the swift, chill waters of a time that flows only one way—to the grave. Our time has become process, historical or personal; process that has no worth beyond what can be realized in some future now. We have lost our right to a home outside of time and so have lost the ability to find a home within time. The passage from life to death cannot be meaningful in a time that flows only into the past. Time as a one-way process has set the bounds to our ability to make good sense of life. Being born and dying—in a nursing home—is the substance of life for us. How can that be an acceptable horizon of life sense?

The Chinese Taoist would understand this and the Confucian too, if differently. The perfection of a past age served the Confucian as truth, not a projected future. The best contemporary musician or thinker brought the beauty and the wisdom of the ancients to life. Time was more a source, holding the past alive to guide the present. Not measured duration, but the treasury of truth. Origins, not destinations, were home for the Confucian.

Our conventional and scientific time is vivially barren set against the Chinese and the Indian understanding. It is a travesty of human life. Yet so far nothing but blanks, questions, and ghosts have turned up to take its place. What if there be no substance to the notion time, if there be no alternative what to measured duration? Perhaps time is not a what. Perhaps the blanks and ghosts were a discovery of time, time as the interweave of iz, waz, and to-be in the now?

Well, word meanings are proving unfruitful. No surprise. Definable, portable meanings are indispensable for some purposes—quantitative thinking, legal interpretations, scientific theory. But time is a living question. Words will have to be used to evoke a lived sense of what is being said, not definitions. Not quite sure what this entails. For now this much is clear: the sense we have of past, present, and future is the way we live them. That sounds like a tautology, but I won't believe it is. True, it doesn't show that the ways we understand time words depends on nameable behavior modes. So, the question: are there ways of behaving typical of each of the three aspects of now? Must try it out.

The brambles are thick grown here, and there may well be some circular errings before there is much clarity. Of course, all behavior izes in the present. So remorse, hope, gratification are in that respect not distinctive of time modes. It will be the intentional outreach of an act—remorse to the waz, hope to the to-be, gratification to the iz—that marks the modes of time. Remorse as a kind of behavior derives from an act committed in some previous present and now living in the waz. One can't experience remorse except as one lives the waz integrated into the iz. So remorse discovers the waz and its power. The feeling of regret for past deeds carries the same sense in a milder way. Guilt is even more deeply rooted in waz. Kierkegaard's Christian sense of sin, and Heidegger's pagan sense of guilt, and even Sartre's "bad faith" are the uninvited burden of an irremediable past. As behavior they further discover the nature of waz and how it is alive in the present. So far all right.

Then there is humiliation, like all feelings known from its izing, but that characteristically descends on one from the rear, in memory. What may have seemed to be annoyance, anger, or defeat at the time can become, as the underlayers of the incident surface, humiliation. Sadness, whatever its immediate object or occasion, discovers something from the past, whether as memory of some loveliness now faded or some expectation unrealized. It will usually, not always, tell the reason for its own existence—the passing season, the absence of friends, the evanescence of one's dreams—and is usually waz's comment on iz.

Remorse, humiliation, guilt, sadness as behaviors rest on the imperturbable authority of the waz. Waz flows in their very veins. Without waz most human behavior would seem quite mad.

No less is the nature of to-be exposed by everyday behavior. Wouldn't excitement—not excitability as a disposition—be meaningless except as reaching out to the uncertain? It presumes an optimistic view of what could happen, unlike fear, but essentially it is our way of living in a promising future that still must be secured in an iz. Fear too lives in an uncertain future, but with a heavy presumption of failure and pain. Joy—not triumph—is of a virtually certain future that promises only good things. It rolls from present to future and helps establish their close interweave. Hope is unthinkable without the uncertainty of the future. If fear expects something bad, hope expects, but does not count on, something good. Such feeling behavior tells us that we have neither complete knowledge nor control of the future, but that it is born of our power of helplessness in the present. So the feelings of hope, fear, joy—and so many others—turn the interdependence of future and present inside out. It is not simply that the future subtends from the present, but that the present is in part created by the future. And so something is learned.

Feeling behavior of the present must focus on what one believes to be the actual, either accepting it or fighting it and thus confirming its actuality. Acting itself confirms the actual, being an expression of confidence, not in the outcome, but in the sure relevance of act to circumstance. If all is well, an act expresses a feeling of rightness, even of completeness or achievement. If all is not well, if one's sense of injustice or ingratitude is sharp or if one's values are endangered, indignation or anger will intend to change the actual. Inseparable from the sense of the actual is the sense of "this is right here". A "spatial" feeling that is the most pervasive mark of the actual and the iz. So, against probability, there is feeling behavior distinctive of the present.

Some feelings of course float freely from to-be to iz to waz. Pleasure, pride, pain, admiration don't speak consistently of one more than another.

But feelings are the sharp edge of our behavior, not the whole cutting blade. Underlying them, dispositions control their range. One person may have a lesser range for anger than another, but a greater range for sadness. They are a more stable factor of behavior than feelings. How could we plan activities, make promises, plot revenge, trust our memories, without, usually unawarely, relying on stable attitudes and dispositions? How else could we live into the not-yet? Still, dispositions cross the path of a time exploration only as individual peculiarities. There is no reason to believe they alter the ways past, present, and future are bonded in the now. But they do affect the importance one gives to its three elements. The cynic may draw more on the past; the optimist more on the future; the organization man more on the present. Some of us find paradise in the past—the Chinese; some find utopia in the future—ourselves; some live in the present—the Buddhists. That would be an interesting study but it is not germane to the problems of the now as time.

More promising is the deep structure of consciousness that holds past, present, and future together more as one phenomenon than three. It has no name, but is an enabling condition of the possibility of human experience. Feelings and ideas told much about the ways past, present, and future are bonded in the now of time. But now is more than a time phenomenon. It is a life phenomenon. We live in the now. If we let our probing awareness sink inwardly into the depths of this very moment, what might we see? Isn't it one round drop of consciousness, full of sense because it seems to be complete as if fulfilled in the future, though not yet; as if illuminated by the past, though not dead; and as being in the present? That is a little preposterous, but what can words do?

There is some evidence to be had, clues really, from experiences in the everyday that allow this to be credible. A closer look at the way iz and to-be can be seen as inseparable. To-be holds open the possibility of completing an iz act. It validates the intention of the act; no responsible act would be thinkable without it. It completes the meaning of an act, the kind of act it is—revenge, apology, promise—by allowing the intention to be as self-assured as the act itself. To-be izes as the great openness that every act is moving toward or indeed is moving in. To-be is the possibility of the worth of acts. Iz feeds timelessly on the to-be. To-be is something like the innate confidence we all have that what we do, in the very doing, already fulfills itself in what is yet to-be. Realization is of course another thing. But iz and to-be make sense only together. Each is nothing without the other. And waz is in the whole of each now of life too. The ease, the confidence with which the inner pulsion of an act arises: how could that be credited to an iz that has no experience? Every moment in the now must draw its stability, its substance from being not a newborn babe, but an ancient citizen of life. That unaware sureness of what is, or should be, or is wanted can't be understood without the live presence of past experiences—the waz. It cannot be absent. It is integral to consciousness. It's so retiring, so everpresent we seldom attend to it. Memories are content of the waz, but not the way waz is one with iz and to-be in the live now.

Great and small, that appears to be the way of things. Waz feeds on the greatness of the past. What we know of past civilizations is of the substance of waz. Unobtrusively, the Egyptian pyramids, the Greek temples, Rome, the lives of Buddha, Socrates, and Jesus form the strongest curve in the horizon of our iz. Waz is the iz's backbone and source of sense.

And iz? Iz is self-evidently more than the base of to-be and waz. Iz says, "Right here is where it's all at. The actual is here. Life is here. Reality is here. Self-awareness happens only here."

Intricate this question of time's now. Or is it now's time?

Once again, and with heightened annoyance, the objector breaks in. Why do you talk only of experiences—feelings, attitudes, ideas? You make time merely subjective. Have you forgotten that time is objective, universal, mathematically measurable, the order of all processes¿ The old confusion arises again. Our time units—seconds, minutes, and so on—are human conventions. We could lengthen or shorten them as we wished. But they may be applied to any process in nature, minute or great. We mustn't mistake invariable repetition in nature—lunar or planetary orbits, the cycle of the seasons—with the nature of time itself. Repetition is not an element of time, however finely we apply our units of time to it. That is clear to me.

In any case, the exploration of now as where we find time discovered no fixed quantities of it. How could it¿ Now is a mode of human experience. It is not "subjective"! There is nothing that could be its object. Past, present, future are the way humans live. They are a major element in any concept of life. Still, this doesn't contradict my objecting friend. Natural processes accept our time words as readily as our own experiences do. This spring's planting of red pine seedlings is now what was; their maturity is in the to-be. This is not a projection of subjective states onto a natural process. It is the way humans must live all process. The human sense of time gathers in all nature to a vivial embrace.

Ah, that vivial embrace. Sounds innocent, feels innocent. But it's as complex as most embraces. It includes the now obviously and should, one might hope, ensure its reliability. But how could it¿ Now focuses passing experience with or without, mostly the latter, an explicit vivial sense. Now is the carrier of all our feebleness and ignorance. And as well the locus of our clarity and good will. It can make nonsense of life.

Nietzsche showed us how memories are, in the nature of things, distortions. Waz, if our source of wisdom, is as much a cavernous archive of self-deception and falsity. Every effort to search for wisdom there must hold its own against the insistent wishes and ignorance of the iz. Falsifications of what once ized return as believable in the form of memories. How could there be a true memory of lived situations¿ What can waz is only one's personal version of the original experience. When distorted memories become the substance of behavior into the to-be, their power to do mischief is the greater for being doubly concealed. To-be is the openness only of a severely enclosed iz. How could it be otherwise¿ To-be is allowed to iz only in ways tolerated by an iz burdened with obsessions disguised as social and personal ideals.

This is black. But it is the human predicament. I believe. If only waz and to-be could be tested and interpreted against some order of things independent of them. But what order? Each is a picture of itself. So we humans must live in a world where falsity crouches behind every assertion of truth and every profession of honesty. And yet out of this predicament comes the poet's and philosopher's sense of the rarity of human life. A rarity that is not destroyed by the distortions of the everyday now.

That's about as much as I'm going to discover about now as time and time as now for a while. It's been an unsettling exploration. I've learned more about what time isn't than about what it is. The three modes of time have transparenced and discovered themselves to be essential to every aware experience. But not as phases in a time sequence nor as distinguishable elements of existence. Each needs the other two to be what we say it is. All three must be present if any one is to fulfill its function in making experience possible. One could say that past, present, and future are words that name nothing. And yet each remains unmistakable. Jolting.

And this: *if* past, present, and future are within now—and they are—then time must be within now. *If* time is composed of past, present, and future. Doesn't sound right. Is now another word for time? If now is not in time, what is it in? It cannot be a second temporal sequence of before and after. Two times! Absurdity would snap if stretched that far.

One paradox after another. Of course paradoxes can be clarifying. At least it's sure that time words have failed to show the way to substantial realities. They have lured me, and disclosed on the way that they gain their meanings from the feelings, ideas, and attitudes they evoke. Time as behavior? Sounds a little too conclusive. Time is still a ghost.

The Non-Now

At this point there's little more to do than note the plain fact that there is so much more to the mighty word time than past, present, and future. And now does not cover much of that much more. We say "Now—but not forever." It is the "forever" that now does not swallow up. Not every experience is lived in the world of past, present, and future. The most ordinary periods of concentration are not lived as izing in the now. They are removed to where there is no awareness of now, to what might be called the non-now, except for the unvivial negative. When a fresh idea seizes one's attention, for a moment there is no awareness of the to-be or waz and so of no explicit iz and so of no now, and hence of no time. By every account of fishing, dancing, singing, meditating, the artist, layperson, or monk experiences the qualitative uniqueness and intensity of what he or she is doing, but without this being borne by a now. There is no sense of before and after. In meditation practice even the novice quickly becomes aware of nothing but breathing—not in and out breathes, but simply breathing—suspended in its own reality. The poet and musician give the same account of moments, even hours, of concentrated writing or composition: no sense of time, inside or outside of now. Indeed it must be one of the commonest experiences for all humans considering the vocabulary available to describe it: "I lost all track of time," "time stopped," "my mind was miles away," "I have no idea where the time went." Gardening or reading or watching a movie commonly brings passages of concentration that we say are "out of time".

That we frequently withdraw from the awareness of now and its izing as to-be and waz, often without effort and at times with some degree of control, unfolds the problem of time generously. Returning to now, one senses clearly that one has been absent. Any experience that overthrows the normal enterprises of the now—ecstasy, fear, absorption in a personal treasure: snow-storm, wind in the forest, loving person—rings in a qualitative substance that is so self-rooted, so self-bringing, so free of cause or explanation that we accept it as immune to the misfortunes of the perishable. We say, on reflection, "It was out of time."

What to make of this kind of experience that won't fit docilely into a now world and tells us bluntly that now is a fragment that cannot be understood by itself? Broaden the view.

The experience of now, it appears, is far from exhausting all aspects of life, and is nonetheless the opening vouchsafed us into the conundrums of existence. If now did not bind our experiences into one field of sense through the interfusion of past, present, and future, we would be condemned to the futility of trying to make sense of senselessly fleeting "moments". Now is the way life presents itself to us prima facie and is the possibility of the question of vivial sense arising. The reflections that move us toward whatever our best sense of life is going to be must establish themselves in the fields of now. Yet sense in the now must be able to embrace non-now experiences even in non-now language. That must be so, but how can it be?

There are so many "best senses" of life. It need not be the existentialist view that human existence is a "living toward death", or the naturalist view that human existence is always and only in now time, or the religious view that life in now is completed and justified by a vaster realm of the non-now.

The puzzlements that lie behind the now will not evanesce easily. Now cannot be a resting place for aware behavior; it is not originally innocent. The interpenetration of now's iz, waz, and to-be may be left in its own intricacies. The demands of the everyday are well cared for by now's mysterious powers of memory, foresight, and action. But now can offer no further help when a question arises that lies outside of memory, foresight, and action: the question whether one can ask the question, "Is there, beyond the kind of sense discoverable in the now, a larger sense that embraces the non-now as well, which presumes a wholeness to life not given in the now, a sense that could be called a life sense?"

Let me get this clear. The active pursuit of a sense of life that would allow one to live out the best that one can expect for humans takes place, as all action does, in the now. All right. But the need of a life sense does not arise from within the now. It is not concerned with the infinitely mutable truths of the now, but with an attainment that could not be comprehended in the terms of now behavior. The question implies asking after the source of the need to arrive at a sense of life to live by. It's not a theory of the way things really are that is in question, but a sense of the way of things; that is, a sense of the best way to take life. And that, it has just become clear to me, would require validation of experiences beyond the time problem. The question is unavoidable but premature. It is now clear: nothing answers to the word "time" in either now or non-now experience, each taken by itself. How could there be? They are two fragments, posited for purposes of exploration.

Why should they make a whole? Yet there are no fragments in life, so how are they held together? And could that tell me anything further about time? I hope it can, for time is still a mighty word. Without it we could say nothing of life at all.

Non-now experiences suffer much from our grammar, from the implied reciprocal negation of now and non-now. There is more to the absorption in a treasured idea, thing, or person than the absence of an explicit now awareness. Experiences without now awareness are just as clearly recalled as now experiences and usually more forcefully. There is no rupture of consciousness. It's the absence of the incessantly restless din and confusion of now's action decisions, uncertain anticipations, personal ambitions, of hoping for more than is certain, and of bad faith with oneself, that marks the difference. Oddly, non-now continues its own kind of action throughout. Bodies continue to move unawarely in dancing, playing musical instruments, in meditational breathing, or gathering in the worth of the day in a canoe on a calm lake in the evening. And the mind continues to touch its favorite images and feelings even in the absorption of the poet or composer. The difference lies in the virtual absence of izing, of resolute decisions, of purpose and will from the non-now and the dominance of an unchanging, single, whole quality. Of course they are not two sealed compartments. Within now there is frequent if faint lessening of iz action, refreshing moments slip unobtrusively in and out of the active mind. And the non-now need not be, though it often is, uninterruptedly clear of passing incursions from now.

We commonly describe the non-now as enraptured, unchanging, peaceful, perhaps as release. What the *Bhagavad Gita* says is an interesting commentary. It makes the difference not a matter of time, but more a difference in existential stance. Now behavior is understood in the *Gita* as action with the primary intention of fulfilling one's desires. This is said to be the self-fueling of the everyday. The *Gita's* alternative to this is not parallel to my non-now, but its emphasis on the possibility of behavior that performs the tasks of the everyday—those of householder, soldier, priest—without the purpose of realizing one's personal desires, is one way of understanding the non-now. Its absorption in what is not the pursuit of one's own interest is a sharp difference from the incessant restlessness of now. It doesn't feed on the uncertainty of one's own successes in the future.

Now and non-now cannot be held apart, memory and dreams bind them, even if nothing else does. Each by its nature reaches out to the other and seeks to penetrate it, to integrate it into its own field of behavior. Each challenges the other. Now's imperial claims are challenged by the abiding disinterest of the non-now, by its demonstration that our most treasured experiences owe nothing to the three queens of now and their turbulent court. Now will understand non-now's discovery of worth outside of now's striving as rest, respite, or perhaps as defeat, mystery, or delusion. It lacks the power to integrate it otherwise. Non-now returns to the turbulence of now hardly believing survival possible there. Now's demonic struggle seems ignorant striving for what is misconceived. Its energy is a potential for its own transformation. There is latent wisdom there that wants only self-awareness. Neither now nor non-now has the power to integrate the other fully, they must share the field of life.

Hegel and Kierkegaard don't help me much here. Both oppose eternity to the finite succession of time and of course vanquish time in the moment of eternity's presence. Presto! As philosophers they may presume the truth of the terms of their dichotomy and allow themselves a quasi-religious pronouncement. Postphilosophically I have no such privilege.

Now and Non-Now Integrated as Story

I have just the question, How do now and non-now share the vivial field? Grammar must become silent. Now and non-now are not a dichotomy of sense, but a tandem of words guiding my vivial interest. Mustn't forget that there is only one sphere of life sense, however many false horizons and concealed contours it may hold. That's my belief. But a sure access to it has been blocked by the sharp disjunction of now, with its ghost of time as succession, and non-now, with its ghost of the timeless. These are so far unsolvable mysteries. But not theoretical problems. The field of human behavior is woven of mysteries. That there should be human behavior is a mystery. Ghosts can be needed companions.

But the two ghosts? What allows all possible sense to integrate into life sense, not as a system but as a field of behavior? As it must if life sense is to be what it says it is? And as I must presume it does if I am to go on searching for it?

Is it the ceaseless turmoil of desires and ambitions, of overt acts, of feelings, pretenses, resolves, of more overt acts, of remorse, of heroism, of understanding, of the occasional discovery of treasures rich enough to salvage some human dignity from ignoble scramblings? Is it this incessant interweave of one experiential substance with another? What else? Sense comes to life from the dependence of one experience, for its happening and its understanding, on other experiences. This dependence is misunderstood as causal; it's rather that experience coheres in dependence. Experiences—what other word is there—come and go in the interdependence of their substances. And this tends to adopt a simple order the more it is repeated, the more it is offered in story or teaching: the order of "this before that", "that after this". To see the interweave of experiences as before and after one another aids in grasping the interdependence of their substances: the gesture of help and the smile of appreciation; the harsh word and the twinge of withdrawal. Even when the order of dependence is, for practical purposes, abstracted into "succession in time" or "causality", it is the dependence of substance that binds experiences together. How helpless we would be if we could not link today's snub from the children with an admission of one's own arrogance yesterday. This is not very Kantian, but so it will seem to me.

Even the most bizarre experiences of mystics—Christian, Muslim, Hindu, Buddhist—are recovered in now and some account of them is given, usually as a story. There is a need to integrate their enlightenment or discovery of god or of oneness with all things—each quite unintelligible in itself—with their path of preparation, wayward or devout, with the trials of anger, doubt, apostasy that led to their clarified moments. The telling of all this, the passing on to their families and followers a relivable account of their journey, seems naturally to take the form of a story, not a theory, not an explanation, but an epic adventure. Offered as a teaching, it attempts to show the interdependence of different experiences, which are of lesser, which of greater life worth. This is the interweave of now and non-now behavior that structures their story. Even hard-headed Nietzsche made a story out of his writing of *Zarathustra*. The pictured person of Zarathustra possessed him so effectively it was as if he himself was not composing the text.

Is the ghost of time coming out of the closet? Succession—before and after—did not offer an intelligible account of the lived now and was put aside. But it wouldn't go away. It has returned, no longer as a definition of time, but as an indispensable element of understanding the meaningful relations between experiences in a story. That is, of grasping their sense. Before and after has become the substantial interdependence of experiences. It seems to be a human behavioral response to the incessant, momentary perishing of all things. The "after" becomes understandable, relivable, because of what happened "before"; and yet it throws its light back to the "before" and illuminates it, makes it more understandable. And the "before" throws light on the "after" but acquires its full sense only from what happens "after". That means the heart of the "after" is in the "before" and of the "before" in the "after". They are inseparable, so neither is intelligible without the other. Neither can *be* without the other. No story could be told unless this were so.

And no mere succession of musical notes could become a melody if it weren't so. We could not interpret certain sounds reaching our ear as a passing automobile or a helicopter coming in to land. We could not appreciate the grace of a dance episode if its movements were related to each other merely in abstract succession. It is so with the episodes of one's own life or any life one tries to understand. Childhood, university, career, family life are not facts strung together on a thread of abstract succession. Rather, their substance, their worth within the interweave of an entire life allows them to make a life story. Succession can aid in discovering the significance of episodes and phases. The life of our year is no different. A succession of four seasons, abstracted from the interdependence of their natures, may delude us into believing we have found time. But the substance of each season appears only when all are held together in one year: only when the silent sleep of winter is lived together with the life of spring, and the burgeoning growth of summer becomes the fulfillment and celebration of autumn, when the need of returning to rest in the coming winter arises. This is not one-way dependence though our calendar encourages us to think so. Winter's nature can be known only through spring, spring through summer, and summer through autumn. Each through all the others, in both directions. The year becomes one life, not a succession of seasons.

The story of human history tells the same. In the West we allow classical Greek and Roman civilizations to be followed by the Dark Ages when they were largely forgotten, and these by the rediscovery of the classics in the Renaissance and this to be gloriously followed by the growth of science and modern Western civilization. But what makes Greek and Roman life "classical", except that later centuries turned to them as models? That is, later periods *made* them classical? And what makes the Renaissance the beginning of the modern West except that later centuries developed in a continuous spirit from then on? That is, the later centuries lend their significance to the earlier, make them what they are in our historical story. Even as we understand the later developments in their dependence on the earlier. The significance of the substance moves in both directions.

Well, succession is hardly the paradigm of time. There is so much more to time's mystery. But before and after is still essential. Without it experience could never be a story. With it alone, time is reduced to the ticking of clocks.

So, the everyday sequence of future, present, and past in the now is gaining some vivial worth. It cannot be got rid of. It's indispensable to our being able to live through days and years on the binding thread of a meaningful story. It is one condition of the possibility of vivial sense. But what of the non-now? It seemed to bring a floating ghost with it, commonly called the "timeless". Not only the great ones, but we ordinary mortals have experiences without any awareness of the now's three phases. This is not insurmountable. Only in theoretical respect are time and timeless, finite and infinite irreconcilable opposites. But not so behaviorally, they interpenetrate naturally. Non-now experiences can, must, yield their sense for life in the now. Otherwise they would be dodos, irrelevant. Preparatory discipline in the now makes the non-now possible and gives the means of understanding it. Behaviorally the two ghosts become one.

But some are adamant. They insist that the timeless is a second realm—the eternal—quite apart from the everyday now and incapable of appearing there. This can be theory and has been a popular one. But it cannot be realized in our living. Any talk of such a separate realm would require a second language, which we lack. And it implies the necessity of two kinds of life, which would be indigestible. Humans find it impossible to make complete sense of one life. Two realms of sense would require two separate beings, which humans aren't. The eternal as infinite time is equally irrelevant. It is either absurd or offered as fine poetry. We talk of truths that will hold "forever": infinite time. But this cannot be lived. It arises from taking clock time realistically and imagining the chain of minutes extended into the future endlessly, and into the past also. This can be said, but it cannot be thought and cannot be lived. It is a fantasy. A human can live only one life story. Whatever the non-now experience seems to say, it must fracture life harmfully if it cannot make its significance felt in the sphere of now.

The great ones have been in no doubt about that. Each tells a story that binds now and non-now into one field of vivial sense. Each has his way of placing special importance on certain kinds of now experience. Aristotle's creative thought, the highest human activity, was also the mark of divinity. Plato's idea of the good was not a moral value but an assertion that the highest worth is the ultimate truth of things. Buddha's simple statement, "The imperishable has been attained," stands for the same. None of these places its emphasis on eternity as infinite time. It is the supreme worth discovered in the non-now that is important.

However that worth is passed on, it naturally gives itself as what needs no cause to explain it. It exudes worth to things of now. It is the touchstone of all worths, not at the mercy of any now. And so it is immune to destruction, imperishable. It is not eternal, infinite time that they discover. It is not that some reality will persist forever, but that the discovered worth is so precious it cannot be destroyed by anything. One might say that the *worth* is timeless. Do we not all believe that about our own discoveries: Wordsworth's Presence encountered in the evening vale; Thoreau's odor of a water lily; an honest moment with one's god; the presence of a loving person? The worth of such moments, not their content, can never die. That is, they form the heart of one's life sense, not as dogma, but to be lived. At every minute and from all sides we integrate our non-now worths, however modestly, with the infinite complexities of our now living. But the plain sense of this is that the content of non-now discoveries can't be conceded ontic substance; it's not the reality of another world. To hold that it is would make it unlivable, a mere dogma. Imperishable worth does not reside in a realm outside the only life humans can live.

How many powerful stories we have of the ways the seemingly transcendental lends meaning to the everyday: the hebraic story of genesis and God's covenant with his people; Plato's account of the cosmic journey of the human soul before birth; Kant's grounding the validity of God and immortality in our experience of the moral ought; Hegel unfolding God's plan for the world. Each is a profound story. Each shapes the possibilities of human life.

Is it mere semantic convenience that I use the notion of story to make some sense of the sequence inherent in future, present, and past and of their substantial interdependence? And some sense of the way experiences from the non-now cohere easily, if unintelligibly, with the future, present, and past of the now? No. Not if this exploration is worth anything. Our everyday, inarticulate sense of things draws us naturally to coherent, that is, meaningful, sequences, which in turn easily bear a sense of the worth of non-sequential experience. Even when the story opens out to tell the destiny of the cosmos, beginningless and endless. We need no infinite time for the story, just the sure embrace of acceptable sense. How else lcan we make sense out of irreconcilable opposites: time, eternity; finite, infinite; intelligible, unintelligible? The story brings its own sense.

Does this mean the story is in time? Definitely not. Is time then in the story? Definitely not. Time cannot consume time. It is the human ability to make sense of life that allows a story to take shape. This ability presupposes the openness that we call a "sense of time" even though we never encounter time. This openness is an essential condition of our ability to make sense out of the whole human story; better, of our presumption that there must be some sense to it. The plain, everyday word "time" stands for the absent presence of an embrace that allows life sense to take form. It leads us to see the need for a horizon from which life sense as story echoes back to us. "Time" is not a name for certain concepts or realities. It preserves the mostly unaware sense that human life has a shaped openness that is not of its own making. Life sense is then aware behavior within one's story of life. "Time" is a great behavioral word.

And that's where I'll leave time for now, about where I left space. The two are inseparable. Space became the unbounded—vivially, not spatially. Time has become what allows the unbounded to assume a form that makes it possible to integrate all experience into one story.

"Time" has been a great teacher. It lead from the clocks and calendars of the everyday—time as an infinite tapeworm sectioned into minutes and years for our convenience—to what allows human experience to cohere in sense. It once again left the everyday as a mask, distorting vivial sense yet somehow revealing what it conceals.

"Time" is the condition of the possibility of life sense. But does not provide its content, though everything—our highest gods, our most precious values, our finest theories—can reach us only by the grace of "time". In our age there is no way to ground dogmas. Beliefs we can have. They are grounded in the imperatives of behavior. Superstitions—children of the gullible everyday—we have, as abundantly as any other time. But dogmas are not our right.

WORDS

How Do We Live With Words?

There is an absurdity in what I am doing from which I must remove the surd. "Inner" and "outer," "space," "time" are mighty words. Ought they not come to us with stable character and meaning? What to make of our language if they don't? How would one express oneself understandably? How be sure what one is trying to say? How indeed. Inner and outer, space, time, when pursued into vivial territory, all failed to yield not only fixed meanings but any wordable meaning at all. Yet they served to evoke a sense that could be experienced. How could they do that, after what they claimed to stand for evanesced into its opposite? If "measured space" is merely the mask of the unbounded and "objective time" is a failed attempt to tell a story that is not in "time", by what logic does it make sense to continue using such everyday words? By none. Ancient habit and natural belief give permission to anthropologists and Humean empiricists perhaps, but not to someone testing our biggest words for their life sense. Must words always mock us with a pretense of meaning that metamorphoses into its opposite under the fingers of inquiry? The realist says they cannot, or we would have no language. Right. At least not one based on defined and unchanged word meanings. But the language we speak is not so based.

Yet we are not gifted to think, to explore, to exist socially without using words. Words are at the center: words. So what are words? How do they function in our daily comings and goings, and in poetry and philosophy? Are they dictionary or computer items, complete with an identity tag called their "meaning?" They have not always been. Ancient Indians, Greeks, Chinese were sure there was more to words than definitions. Some thinkers in every age have experienced language as a gift to humans beyond their devising. Others have tried to explain human speech as a natural function, like building a house. Today human speech is under an assault on the broadest front ever, the more deadly for not being recognized. It is not recognized because the assault flies splendid banners: "information," "communication," "computers in every classroom"—as well as picture machines that inhibit the use of words. How preserve the precious spontaneity of genuine speech in this jungle?

Our highest values threaten it most. Egalitarian, computer democracy is so rigid in its ideas that speech must conform, and people too. We are thing minded, and common language is a string of thing words. We are so good at making and selling things that the air around pullulates with their names and virtues. And so our talk flattens to the metallic character of advertising slogans and television news—not much difference. We swim in oceans of words. We eat and drink them and spit and laugh them out again incessantly, from and into radios, speech machines, videos, telephones. Little wonder Samuel Beckett longed for a language of nonwords and vowed to punch holes in the facade of the language we use, to see what is hidden behind it. My feeling exactly. But how justify it? How else but by coming to see what words are, how they function for us, what wonderful things they can do and what wonderful things they cannot do; and how far they vitiate themselves by false expectations? Very especially, to see in what way they can be used to explore what lies behind words. And what we do about it if they cannot be.

The positivist grasp of language in our own time—as docile subject matter for logical or commonsense analysis—is unreal and of little help. Except that it reminds how easily we make the fateful assumption about words: that they are given to us, as they are in their innocence, without possibility of error. Even for the postmodernists, the problems of language seem to begin *after* words have offered themselves to the expert for study. Commonly we treat words as citizens of a special domain, where their sole function is to carry "meaning" or "significance".

But words are alive and human for the postmoderns. One can't say that for the merchants of "communication theory." Has the machine ever shown its power over the human mind more than in the belief that language is the "means of communication" between one human and another? Even the assumption that language *is* communication derives its sense from the machine model of the telegraph, telephone, radio, and computer. This view demands that words have definable, packageable, portable meanings—tidy, machine-coined pieces of information. A demand that blankets out their precious spontaneity.

One day language must escape from the hypnotic trance layed on it by the positivists, speaking from their scientific, egalitarian, one-dimensional world. Their assumption of the naturalistic origin and factualness of words blots out the ancient wisdom of appearance and reality. Words are their last court of appeal. What inner and outer, space and time have shown me makes that dogma seem empty and quite useless in exploring for life sense. Words are more a pervasive mystery. They conceal, behind their well-groomed logical behavior, character complexities that make logic look naive.

So, for me words remain a mystery. Once again the elemental questions arise. What are words for? What do they do for us that unworded experience does not do? Are there experiences without words? Why must we so often struggle to find the "right" word? Why are words not given with an experience? Do words deceptively confer reality on the everyday, as the Buddhists think? Or are they the only wings of enlightenment we have, as Herder holds: language alone giving form to the inner being of humans? Are words, as Heidegger has it, "the house of being"? Do words behave the same way in the everyday as they do for the poet or the philosopher or the religious person? Is their primary service the preservation of meanings? Or do they mesh with behavior other than as meanings?

So many questions! Questions are easy. I'll not find answers to them, just like that. But need questions be answered, to be good questions? What if the initial questions lose themselves in better questions? If they do, so be it. A life sense exploration of words is more than a little presumptive, clearly. Yet it can't be circumvented. I'm not asking, what are words? But, how do we live with them? What can they can tell me about the best way to make sense of all things?

Language needs words. And words are used mostly as names,

it seems. The everyday world is a kind of forest of named things that surrounds each one of us. Naming things makes social action possible and saves pages of gesticulation. In the ordinary course we don't confer reality on anything unless we can name it. Names and the network of things correspond so flawlessly, that for the greater part, we remain unaware of the difference. Our seldom expressed but firmly held natural belief is that things *are* what they are called. The name penetrates the whole of the thing. An apple is an apple right through. Names present themselves as things. It's that simple. The English farmer thought the French, though polite, very ignorant, because they called their horses "chevoh" when everybody knows they're horses. Words enlarge our personal worlds. We talk about things we have never experienced, but we pay for this, because names delude ruthlessly. Being simple themselves they mask the complexity of things. They conceal those aspects of things that are turned away from our habitual uses and interests. What intricacies the simple name "eyeball" conceals, yet how successfully we use it everyday.

One can even say that names—"eyeball," "head," "body," "earth"—do not name the thing they lead us to because, being composed of many parts, no one of which is the thing named, nothing in the thing answers properly to the name we call it by. Names are the wallpaper of our worlds. They determine not only the colors and patterns around us but the kind of reality we live in: one of surfaces turned toward ourselves: turned toward our interests, our purposes, our prejudices, our aversions, our ignorances. Oh names! You slavish servants.

If this is so, words don't name a world of outer things and their properties quite unrelated to the humans maneuvering among them, in spite of our determination to think they do. The symbiotic interdependence of outer and inner is brought home strikingly in our use of words. Things take their place in the action spaces of a human world as their names tell their importance for the life needs and desires of humans. We respond to outer things, and things receive their worth from our inner desires and needs.

Each small inlet in the great ocean of language is molded to evoke and accommodate the behavior of those who live on its protected shores. A fishing village, turned out in fisherman's language, is so attuned to the needs of boats and people and fish that one can read the village as a textbook for fisherman's behavior. As though the benamed things carried the longings of humans; as though human longings could read from the worded things the behavior appropriates to them.

So, there is sense in saying that names do not define or describe, odd as that sounds. They can't, it seems; indeed, are not meant to. Though we commonly believe they are. Names lead us up to the things that are important for us, but are not what we interact with. A thing's complexity and uniqueness must escape a name—*eyeball*—used for countless similar complex and unique things. Dignaga said it long ago, "A name is not what we seize on in action." Names are masks, Nietzsche told us. Names seem to stand between us and the things we seize on in action.

Language as a computer full of names is a parody, of course, but not a fabrication. Words do tumble out of our mouths very often in reflex action, without thought or feeling. And in so many decisive life situations words are not only a wallpaper pretense of reality, they block access to hidden feelings and the silent nature of things. That morning Susan jolted my complaisance by saying of her 10-month old boy, "No, he hasn't started to talk yet. I dread the day when he does, because then we'll not be close to each other any more." The heavenly gift of language a barrier between people! An inferior mode of being with another human! Of course Susan was right. Did everyone know that but me?

That chance remark made the radical otherness of words and what words are about the more striking and puzzling. Words seem grown together with inner states and outer things to which they are wholly alien. The word "feeling" is itself not a feeling; the word "love" is from another universe than love itself. Words are air, sound, hollow, of another nature than the living things we apply them to. All our lives we talk to our own ideas and feelings and to the people and things around us, and all we have is a handspun web of words; words that distance us from our own feelings and the feelings of others, even as they appear to bring us closer; words that mark the forward edge of our ignorance, even as they promise knowledge.

That sounds willfully harsh, but so it is for me. Can I believe the consequence: no word can be true of its object? And the consequence of that: the possibility that speech is condemned to futility, and with it knowledge? That would be a cold plunge. Humans tilting quixotically with windmills built of their own breath, not building "the house of being". Are we that absurd? The question is still open. And the behavior of words will have much to say about it.

At times words are not merely incapable of giving life to feelings and ideas, but seem to destroy the experience they would preserve. Anyone who tries to write must discover this. That winter day so long ago, on a local train grinding its way through the arctic Norwegian mountains. Those overwhelming mountains, engulfing the tiny toy we were sitting in. Darkness seeping in early. My vague apprehension. And then, the lights and life of Narvik! Splendor, perfected by safety! Next morning, that horrible sensation at reading the words I had found the previous evening for the experience of the day. They destroyed it. They shriveled an awesome experience into tasteless commonplaces. They were a violation of what should have been preserved in its own silence. They were more the wrappings of a mummy, or an epitaph.

The season I was alone at the lake. The same thing. But in reverse. With no need to use words, everything moved closer: the bark of the trees, the rocks, the lake in all its moods, the frolicking loons, the sailing clouds, the cope of sky, the vultures wheeling and wheeling, the haunting secret of the moon. All came closer. Their natures came alive and began to speak to me as if I mattered to them. My new-found fellow inhabitants, without names or qualities or poetic overlay, grew in importance and came closer in a friendlier way. There seemed to be nothing between us, no words holding us apart. They were eloquent within a human world and I, mere human, seemed to be a fellow in their world.

These plain experiences insist on a solemn observation: words, as words, don't gather in and hold truth for us. By themselves they lack this power. Only in clarifying our attitudes and refining our behavior do they have some meaning or sense. That sounds overwrought, even strange, but it is not so strange. After all, the greatest thinkers outside of the Greek-European tradition—Taoist, Buddhist, Vedantist—didn't believe that the truth of things was of a nature to be given in verbal statements. Chuang Tzu's dictum, "Words are the guests of reality" says: the eternal Way plays tolerant host to whatever names are conferred on it at different times, but does not admit any name to its permanent household.

Buddhist and Vedantist, both in their own way, say what is quite compatible with that: truth is lived, not spoken. Zen adherents are sure that their truth has been transmitted silently from teacher to student, beyond words, century after century. Nagarjuna and his Middle Way school are closest to what I'm finding out. There is no truth of the way of things except as the enlightened person discovers this through his or her behavior. And this discovery is not a conceptual system, but a discovery of how to live with things. As the wise person takes things, so they are in themselves. Truth, apart from a way of behaving, is simply nonsensical. However, they were sure that words are indispensable guides toward the discovery of the way and help to secure it in the behavior of the wise person, but are neither true nor false apart from that behavior.

This is a powerful thought, so easy to hold in the mind, so contemporary, so compatible with antiphilosophic, antiscientific protest thinking. It says: words obscure the virgin nature of things, laying a thick blanket of everyday presumptions over the true world. And so say I.

But the commonsense realist! Indeed, my own common sense! It cannot be quite like that. The realist is persuasive. "But words are the means of effective social behavior. My husband and I agree to meet at the library at noon. And lo and behold, we are both there at noon—thanks to words naming exact time and places". Thanks to their both being punctual! But when the realist draws in examples from the law courts, business contracts, political realities, the argument seems weightier.

Of course our business and political life depends on a common vocabulary. But consensus in use has nothing to do with the truth of the words used. "Yes it has" the realist insists. "If our words were not true of things, things would frustrate our actions, and tell us plainly that our ideas of them were false. But that seldom happens. Ergo, our ideas as expressed in social vocabularies must, generally, be true."

Oh to be as self-assured as the realists. They're both right and wrong. They're right that our social and political vocabularies are generally adequate for everyday purposes. But this doesn't justify them holding that usage establishes truth. The language of names is socially effective not because names tell us the nature of the things named, but because they serve as guides to bring us into the presence of the things we have in mind and to suggest appropriate action toward them. We are seldom in trouble if we assume that the word "bread" names a specified kind of thing. We can say "pass the bread," "how do you bake bread," "bread isn't good for you," and effectively further the social action intended. So far, agreement. But when one reads dozens of recipes for different "breads"—from whole grain oat bread to quick rise baking powder bread; and in between, "beer" and "papaya" and flat "frying-pan" bread—something has to be cleared up. "Bread" obviously does not name a definable substance, nor is it a true general term. It's a handy word that saves talking and provokes appropriate behavior—so long as the situation of its use is clear to all concerned. That is the crux. The situation brings silent assumptions into play: shared intentions, eating habits, cooking equipment, and family idioms. Within these the word "bread" permits the teaching and learning of how to bake bread, agreeing what bread is in question, who will eat it, how much to make. In no case will one end up with a pie.

It's not different in more sophisticated situations. "University" names no particular thing—universities having become virtual cities within cities. But it never did. And so for "education", "justice", "equality". However polysyllabic the names used, all function in the same way. They are carried by the unvoiced presumptions of the social group using them. And they guide thinking or other behavior into the appropriate regions. They are not one-to-one code names for ideas or things. That much I'm sure of.

The outrage of my learned friends! Especially the idealist. "This is preposterous. What of the learned disciplines: philosophy, history, sociology, theology? They are all based on definable meanings. How else is knowledge possible? To level everything to your pragmatic situations is plain nonsense." Again the protest is justified and misguided. Immanuel Kant, Meister Eckart, Plato were not teaching us how to bake bread. Their words carry universal meanings; they are not limited by a social milieu like cookery or education. True.

And yet, there's no clean break between the everyday use of words and the learned and poetic uses. The accusation of pragmatism is a radical misunderstanding. How get people to see that both commonsense realism and idealism miss the point? Because idea-words are not gold coins clinking together in rarefied conversation, set apart from lower-class feelings, impulses, intentions, preferences, prejudices, resentments that are the bulk and flow of our inner life. Ideas are guests in the mind, honored guests, but still carried by the dynamics of the household of the mind—conscious and unconscious. Every idea-word moves on feeling and value preference and, in deliberate thought, by judgment of its suitability. Everyone can observe this in his or her own mind. Learned conversation and—somewhat differently—poetry and religious expression are, true enough, not limited in their meaning and worth to local social milieus. But they are limited by the scope and depth of the inner milieu of the minds engaged. How can we appreciate what such languages are saying unless their idea-words arouse experiences in us capable of giving the words life, of catching their "sense"? This is not pragmatism. But it's also not accepted theory of knowledge. Some would quote Kierkegaard at me and urge me to admit I'm an idealist, but that would be misleading too. Neither blanketing real things with ideas, nor separating the two is convincing.

How Do Words Function for Us?

The problem is words: how they carry out their functions for us. The temptation is to set up classes of word function. There might be the everyday word. It furthers individual purpose and interest amid the jumble of things surrounding us. It's limited to one's local language, customs, work, and one's own nature. It functions in a "practical" milieu, we say. Everyday words name things and evoke overt behavior. Then there is the use of words to explore questions beyond one's everyday milieu: the nature of society, of science, of history, of philosophy—learned theories in short. Individual interest and prejudice are not absent, most certainly, but are not as openly admitted as in the everyday. Here words evoke *idea* behavior. The common body of learning becomes part of the milieu. And then, still further from the everyday, we often say there is the remote realm of poetry, religious experience, and life wisdom.

Maybe. But such distinctions are artificial to the last word, of course. There can be more life wisdom in the folklore of an unrecorded Himalayan dialect than in Marcus Aurelius. And more thing-bound realism in religious talk than in the mundane conversations of a tribal family. So there are not three levels of word use at all. But the notion reminds of the many different ways words may be used. And that words are not primarily cognitive. So I'll not acquiesce in traditional theories of knowledge and their presumption that ideas have a life of their own in the human mind, a life designed to serve the purposes of knowing.

Against this, it is becoming clear, we humans are normally borne by an undertow of pulsions—aversions or attractions—mostly unaware and below the threshold of names. We say we have intuitions, urges, dumb feelings, forebodings, uneasy guilt, a strong "sense of", and leave it at that, as if these were distant and slightly disreputable cousins. But our unworded inner life is the seat and source of our valuations, of our sense of direction, of unacknowledged decisions, of dim, background images that lend sense to things. We move through problem situations, we arrive where we feel we belong, but didn't know this was where it was. Let this not be called "instinct" or social "programming". It's the wordless discourse each one has with himself or herself in overt action, in explorative behavior, in silent brooding. The unworded voices are the source of our sense of what we are doing, however seldom we become aware of it. And they tell us if we should continue doing what we are doing. But it would be a distortion to say they are cognitive voices. From them comes our sense of what is "going on" not only in ourselves but in the inner of anyone we are with or in whole situations where we are involved. Our intermittent speaking episodes are carried by the steady flow of unspoken pulsions and driftings. It gives speech its possibilities and its purpose. This kind of sense is not gnoseal, having no object to know. It is the undercurrent of speech; unnoticed, it prompts our breaking out into speech and our withdrawal from it. Nietzsche even called this his "great reason". His "little reason", like Chuang Tzu's, survives in language and logic. Sense moves in its own direction, not deciding explicitly, but quietly fending off or being impervious to all suggestions that are not acceptable to it. Something like the Upanishadic "not this", "not that". It's so clear. Yet it sound subversive. Am I odd?

The language semioticists would think so. Their focused concern with those areas of experience that can be exhaustively explored with words passes right by my dumb "sense". What lies outside verbal signification lies outside their problem. Is it their belief that there are no areas impervious to verbal signification? Would they leave human behavior without a foundation? Such a self-imposed closure could only block vivial exploration.

So, in everyday talk situations, the situation itself is absent from the talk. One's sense of what is going on—the unspoken purposes and schemes of the others, interacting with one's own unconfessed, barely conscious motives—though the basis of one's behavior and talk, is absent from the worded surface of the talk situation. Scholarly discussion is not that different. There is always a silently present situation: a senior scholar with students, an outsider attacking the tradition, the acknowledged authority unveiling new ideas. The entire field of discourse—modern history, English literature, law—is the additional unspoken element within which the learned sentences fall. It, too, though absent from the sentences exchanged, is decisive in understanding what is being said.

Can it be that words of life wisdom or poetry—taking the third of my invalid categories—find their sense not in a social milieu, nor in a field of learning, but in an inner openness as large as life itself? When words of wisdom strike they have a bell-metal quality that seems to evoke an echo from horizons beyond the known horizons. Can I risk saying there are words whose sense a person may "hear" as if it resounded from the horizons of life itself? We may think of such life sense as coming from ourselves, but that doesn't make the best sense. So great we are not. A person will be the speaker of life sense and its receiver, but how could one of us emit an echo that is truly life wise? Life sense echoes must be echoes from life—or else they're misnamed. Chuang Tzu's mind stopper: "Benevolence is not benevolent." Don't we have to withdraw behind our best analytical propositions to approach its vivial sense, perhaps: morality is a pompous fraud concealing the Way of things?

This is a difficult but fascinating turn. An understanding is taking over that I do not quite understand. My three types of word use are not of much use. It appears now that they are much more alike than different. In each case, whether everyday or vivial, the words of a sentence are not the source of their own meaning. Understanding is not mechanically one to one. The sense of words comes to one in the echo the words give as they resonate from the silent sounding board of understanding. Mostly it is the sounding boards of personal interest or intellectual curiosity that come into play. But life wise insights can break into our everyday awareness at any time—even if rarely. It must be so. How else relate the human being to life itself? Word processors can't do it. Everywhere the weight of words that is not given in a sentence, but derives from the unworded situation into which they fall or, when it happens, from the resonations of vivial openness is no longer adequately thought of as their meaning or signification. It is their "sense". I hope that makes sense. It will take some explaining. But this much does not: meaning is from a dictionary; sense is from life.

There is another, unfortunately prevalent, use of words that might help fill in the range from the everyday to the vivial: the doubletalk of the salesperson and the politician. What of the political election statement: "Giving $8 billion in extra farm subsidies is not buying votes; it's nation building." Or, "Our nation is winning the race to the future." To catch the sense of such rhetoric is not merely to understand the meaning of the words; nor is it enough merely to realize that these statements are lies. They must be allowed to resound from the nature of democratic politics and from history. And then they tell us that their truest sense is not only absent from the words, but is quite the opposite of their apparent meaning. The first statement then would say, "Massive corruption buys votes, but sets a nation against itself." And the second would say, "Ignorance of human history in high places engenders crippling ignorance among the people."

What relates such talk to life wisdom talk? Well, in both cases, the sense of the words is absent from their meaning. Their sense arrives as an echo from a vivial horizon that itself is nowhere detectable in the occasion of their utterance. To say "sounding board" sounds a little wooden! But it reminds that we sense the worth of the sentence filling the air around us, not from the words themselves so much as from what is missing in them. Of course, the one isn't separate from the other: the very words used carry the unspoken worth that we sense.

The semioticists would hold that the absent sense I'm trying to put my finger on is the signification of the words used—via a network of absent words. Signification is, by its nature, not a fixed part of the word itself. So it must be. But where is the signification summoned from? It is not self-evident that it must be from a network of absent words. What is the logic of the link between present words and absent words? How could there be such? What bridges the gap between "Benevolence is not benevolent" and "Morality is a pompous fraud"? It cannot be word signification, or one could show the logic of the interpretation. But the contradictory variations in the interpretation of such wisdom words make that impossible. My own understanding of Chuang Tzu is obviously no more than just one of these.

So, where is the signification, one's understanding, summoned from? Social milieu, professional learning, political cynicism? Each in its turn. But what happens when it is a question of sentences like Chuang Tzu's? I'm finding that it echoes from an infinitely complex, personally shaped life sense by the grace of which each of us lives. This defines the crux and the challenge: life sense is verbally incalculable. It's not a thing, not a feeling, not an idea. But I talk about it. How understand the way it is related to the words used?

Some life wisdom from the great. "Less is more". "Categories mark the beginning of ignorance". "Words are the guests of reality". Such vivial sentences can't be subjected to a true-or-false inspection. Nietzsche's words, telling us that our highest ideas are not knowledge but the beginning of ignorance, we "understand", if at all, only by recalling his destructive assault on everything that was considered knowledge in his day, by recalling his view that language lays a mask over things, and by recalling that his way of putting the traditional question "What is that?" was "How do I behave toward that?"

Those who believe words are signs will believe Nietzsche's words simply arouse an infinity of linked meanings, all given in other words. But this is misleading. It is not Nietzsche's words that carry the deepest sense of his dictum, it is his rejection of all language for truth purposes. Categories are part of the mask of language. His sense of the futility of words and their specious truth opens up for him the ranges of experience where words are not ready to hand, lulling us into complacency. Nietzsche's sentence releases an awakening to the radical character of life for which no words are available. If words were available they would make Nietzsche's words untrue. One senses in which direction to pursue the consequences of his words; that is, how to take them, how to live with them. We ask, if our best concepts are ignorance then what takes their place? Is there a new kind of knowledge? Or are there other ways of living after the descent of nonknowledge? This kind of exploration does not proceed primarily by the grace of words and their meanings. It proceeds more by grace of a wordless groping, by trusting one's sense of the way Nietzsche's thought is trying to go. Of course, words are flitting in and out of the groping, and helpfully, but as promptings or warnings to our explorations, not as items in a system of signs.

Sense as Life Sense

So, what is this "sense" that lures me into following it? Where does it come from? If it is not worded meaning how can it link up with the public network of word meanings? Two unrelated universes of experience, one worded and one not, makes no sense.

Is sense something like a transmutation at the far reach of the spectrum of meaning? Both lie at the heart of human awareness and behavior. Meaning is more at home in the everyday and sciences. Sense is the way we come closer to the vivial, to the riddles of the human predicament. Neither meaning nor sense can be confined within a network of concepts and their words. Both are borne by interests, purposes, ignorance, and by their behaviors. Those years when I limited myself to writing on the magic of reality. Even though it was clear I was narrowing my sensibilities and lessening my aptness for contemplation. Only some unworded sense said it was better so. How could I be sure I would be any more capable of guiltless contemplation if I gave up the work? It was not word meanings and reasons for and against that brought sureness. Such dilemmas yield only to a sense that comes from living out as deeply as possible the experiences that the words lead to. At times a life question chokes the mind and demands its own solution. If you've been celebrating the falsity of all words and things single mindedly and suddenly turn the coin over to wonder how these very same words and things can be the sole entry into truth, then you discover the impotence of reasoning. To trust in inferential movement on the back of the very words and concepts one has been unmasking as false is hardly convincing, though not unknown. Reasoning unfortunately chokes off all possibilities outside one's presumptions of the moment. Sense is by nature more open. It draws on ways to move that are not suggested by the verbal formulation of the problem. Maybe, with good fortune, it can move with seven-league boots to unsuspected insights; perhaps improper ones, incapable of proof, but still making good sense. Pascal's distinction between reason and the reasonable comes to mind.

The pursuit of the sense of a question is a kind of behaving involving decisions, value preferences, risks. Concepts and word meanings are its fodder. In turn they awaken further sense that fuels further exploration. Meaning, of course, is indispensable, but secondary and instrumental. Sense, the voiceless center of a person, finds the way to go. It both lures one to follow and tests the most promising areas to search in. It helps one to arrive where one thought one might want to be; and, it seems, it is sense one finds there. And it is sense that tells one how to behave toward what one has found. Can so much "sense" make sense? I wonder. But how else say that subject and object are wholly superfluous in this process?

Quantitative space and time yielded to the exploration of their life sense by becoming the opposite of what they seem to be. Space opened out into the boundless, time metamorphosed into the possibility of an unending story. That surprises and even arouses disbelief, but it makes a certain kind of sense. Vivial sense becomes more plausible in the altered behavior evoked by what we discover behind everyday realities. Space as the boundless is lived with other emotions, other imagining, and other thoughts than space as a measurable quantity. So too with time. Entry into a drama, full of life significance but without beginning or end, is a far cry from the ticking of one's wristwatch or the date on one's calendar.

Sense insists on separating itself from word meaning. I must stay with that. But this is the razor's edge: where does sense come from, if not from words? Chuang Tzu: "The understanding that understands nothing is the finest understanding." Such wisdom words can jolt us from the beworded everyday into regions where we have no words left to use. That must be so for every dictum that eviscerates language. Nagarjuna: "Stolen predicates are false; all predicates are stolen." But it is "false predicates" that alert us to the limits of language and hint at what lies behind words. How can words carry a sense that is not given with them?

Nietzsche, Chuang Tzu, Nagarjuna all reaching for the sense of things through verbal paradox. Nietzsche trying to say that our finest theories are ignorance—by enunciating his own theory! Chuang Tzu saying the finest understanding understands nothing—and hopes we understand that! Nagarjuna condemning all predication—by means of predication! Each uses words that contradict the sense he is trying to give them. But they are not the opposite. It's rather that intention fills out the sense of the words, is their compensatory completion. The words appear to destruct their own sense, but make their impact by that appearance.

Even my own feeble paradoxes make the same point: "The most real is the most false." This is non-sense, equating "real" and "false". It defies logical disentangling or semantic articulation. The non-sense just grows thicker. Until the magic of reality dawns on one: our ability to treat as solid-body real what are no more than human postulates required for behavior. "The blue sky above", "the rising sun", "the wind in the trees". Such false realities are not "explained" by a linkage of subtle word meanings. To try misses their vivial worth, which is that they open the door to grasping everyday illusions as integral to our behavioral needs, as deriving their sense from them.

What fine words! Do my own sentences refute my belief? Should I drop the question of sense and word? Well, there is a story about this. Humans live in a boundless habitat that, being human—however many gods share it—must hold some sense for them, if they can find it. Word meanings struggle, but fail, to reach into this vivial sense. Life baffles words. So we resort to paradoxes when we catch a strong sense of the way it is with life. But word-meaning language needn't die on the lips of the speaker, nor at the ears of the hearer, nor in a network of significations. It makes more sense to think that, as are their power and range, so words resound within the boundless human habitat of no beginning and no ending. Humans dwell in a vast echoing space that reforms the spoken sound and returns it as a soundless echo bearing a sense of the way of things. Even if the spoken words made no sense. We give meaning to words that reach the ear; but who else can receive and be affected by the vivial sense of their echo except a human person? It is as though the horizons of human awareness acted as a great sounding space completing those sentences, but only those, that penetrate to them, in such a way that the vivial worth of the sentence is given in the echo. And new possibilities of behavior open up with the echo. That's the best story I know. Of course the "echo" makes sense here only because it is soundless!

The ancient belief that there can be wise persons whose every sentence echoes back from unseen vivial horizons is not bizarre. Was Lao Tzu one such? "What is half will become whole. What is crooked will become straight. What is empty will become full. What is old will become new." The prima facie meaning of these words is banal naturalistic optimism—of no interest here. But if we catch their sense from within Lao Tzu's world as we understand it, then he is saying: "What is half is already whole. What is crooked is already straight. What is empty is already full. What is old is already new." This makes it into a paradox telling how wisdom can transform the everyday face of things by removing individual perspective and prejudice. These are the source of the everyday value judgments "half", "whole", "empty", "full". For the enlightened, each thing in every situation is fulfilled as what it can be there. A seedling is not a whole tree, but it is a whole seedling. A devious plan can aim straight at its purpose.

Can the nature of the human being be understood in these terms? It could be. What other being, as far as we know, carries the aware longing for fulfilment in sense out to whatever it is that responds with an echo? What other being can hear the transformed worth of spoken words? Or is open to the life worth of experiences that have no words? Without words to entangle us in the paradoxical facade of the everyday, and so start the echoes of sense resounding, we wouldn't be human persons.

There's another thought that has only very slowly come into view. If speech is to carry vivial resonance, it has need of something other than itself. Neither the unworded echoes that are needed to complete the sense of even our most clarified philosophic sentences nor the human need for those echoes is a function of language. Yet both are immanent in our speech from the beginning. The powers that make language possible are themselves not lingual.

This is very close to what the Sanskrit Upanishads could say ages ago: "That which is not expressed through speech, but that by which speech is expressed, that is the truth." "What dwells in speech yet is other than speech, what speech does not know, what controls speech from within, that is the deathless truth of things."

Did Heidegger read the Upanishads? He would have felt a strong sympathy. But when the dust settles, deep in the land of thinking, Heidegger has not given up the Greek-inherited belief that human language reaches into the mysteries of Being and is able to find words adequate to what is discovered there. Whereas the Upanishads never forget that words are citizens of the great cosmic realm of appearances and lead us to the experience of truth only as they become transparent.

For myself, it is now clear that word meanings fail to survive in the outer reaches of human experience. They lose their way; they lose the power to penetrate; they evanesce. But in resounding through the great spaces they gather a sense of where they have been and bring it back to us as a vivial echo.

We must suppose that the source of this echo, this new worth, though it lets light into our words, does not itself speak human words. That stretches belief. What is this mysterious source? Well, it is not a "what", that's sure. I am sure only that the experience of the word source keeps the need to understand moving toward whatever in our world is beyond perception, beyond science, beyond knowing. But nothing in the realm of being answers to the name "source". Never. In spite of all temptations! It is a behavioral word, not a name for a transcendental being. It lures to exploration. And it justifies itself, if at all, in the experiences it provokes.

KNOWING

Is Knowing Unintelligible?

If words aren't meant to hold and tell truth, doesn't that deny them any function in the processes of knowledge? Within the Greek-European tradition it would do more than that. It would remove any meaning from the word "knowledge". It would deny its possibility. It is so: from Aristotle to Husserl the presumption that knowledge could be realized only through words with definable meanings was so self-evident it could not be grasped as a mere presumption. Except by fringe skeptics and mystics and Nietzsche, who were ignored in their time.

Not until our own time did this presumption surface as merely that. The way postmodernists have exploited their freedom, though it is new and encouraging, brings too many problems. Words have widely been given over to whatever uses and meanings an individual can turn them to. So long as they carry some significance for writing and speech they need no fixed meanings. And that means the notions of truth and knowledge can be put aside.

So it is. But these aren't the only two possibilities. What if words enable knowing in other ways than as carriers of fixed meanings? And are indispensable to any "truthing", even though they don't possess truth? What if truth and knowledge reach us in other ways than through words? As traditions other than our own have found.

It doesn't seem cogent to say that knowing is an absurdity or an illusion, not yet anyway. "Knowing" is a mighty word. Our language pivots on it. And yet the symbiotic relation of subject and object—inner and outer— is an unpromising background for an exploration of knowing. There is no way around the discovery that the world surrounding us is not an interweave of realities indifferent to our feelings and ideas, as we commonly suppose, nor that all individuals do not carry a second world within themselves, separated from outer realities. Despite its paradoxes, this view is tenable for sense perceptions and feelings and names.

But what about scientific theories? Is knowing a universally valid intellectual operation? The plausibility vanishes. An idea would be inseparable from the object it was an idea of; there could be no object of our knowing separate from our knowing it. There would be no escape from holding that the physical universe was not independent of the theories of physicists, nor living nature of biological theory. That assaults common sense. Have scientific conceptions of things not changed frequently over the centuries? Is nature supposed to have changed with them? But even this apparent absurdity doesn't dissolve the inseparability of inner and outer.

It's our understanding of knowledge that generates the problem. It rests on a profound paradox, which we seldom bother to recall. We believe that the object of knowledge remains what it is, whether it is known or not. The knowing of it does not alter it. If it did, we would have to give up the idea that knowledge yields objective and universal truth. Yet it is plain that we have no power to become aware of the nature of an object independent of our knowing what it is. There can be no description of the supposed independent object other than the description our knowledge of it provides. We have no access to the nature of objects other than the access of knowledge. What second access is there? Wittgenstein put it bluntly: "There is no escape from language to nature."

I wonder. Does knowing have to be unintelligible? Or is it our conception of it that generates the paradox? If we hold knowing to be a unique, autonomous relationship between idea-words internal to a subject and objects perfectly independent of these subjective idea-words, then knowing is forever unintelligible. But could there be ways of understanding knowing that avoid Wittgenstein's dictum? If that is to be possible, the problem will have to metamorphose radically.

The Everyday

The question reaches from the surface of the everyday to the depths of tribal and classical wisdom. The latter is available for study, but what does the everyday say? How do we use the word "knowing"? Do we use it in a simplified version of the scientific and philosophic? Or in ways that stretch the word into other fields of experience?

Well, what do we say we "know" in the vernacular? Each of us knows his or her own name; that is, we can pronounce the name we've been told is ours from childhood. We know our age; that is, we can say what we've been told it is.

I hear myself saying I know a cedar log from a pine log. I know that planet is Mars. I know the name of the prime minister is Laurier. I do not know the name of that tree, nor of the new neighbor. So knowledge in the everyday is an adequate vocabulary! Not quite. Still it's sobering to remember the infinity of knowables lying docilely beneath a name. Beneath anyone's name—a person; beneath the word "mars"—nuclear physics; beneath the words "cedar" and "pine"—a range of biochemistry that takes years to master. Yet names make us knowers, even as they cover over our ignorance.

And then the countless times we affirm our certainty by saying "I know that . . . so and so." I know that the sun is shining. I know that it's 12 o'clock noon. I know that this is my body. I know that I am writing. I know that it's time to plant the garden. Incessantly we mark off a second order of sureness by saying "I know that . . . " Sometimes we may merely *think* it's 12 noon, or that it's time to garden, or that the sun is shining. But if we wish to settle the argument we thrust the word "know" into the discussion: often based on a direct perception, often based on an habitual conviction, often justified. But again it is sobering to recall what profoundly ignorant presumptions can ensure the truth of an everyday saying. Is the sun not shining perpetually whether or not a fluff of moist atmosphere happens to intervene between the spot on the earth where I stand and the sun? Is the loose cluster of legs and arms and torso we point at when we claim to know our own body, really our body? We point at the skin surface of a few large members of an organism so infinitely complex it cannot be described. What we see covers our body. And imagine a nonmaterial wraith like "I" or "me" claiming to possess a part of physical nature! At the very least "my body" is a mystery; at worst it is a nonsense. But it passes in the everyday for something we know. Often knowing says I accept folk wisdom and morality. "I know I should take more exercise." "I know I should vote in the local election." "I know I should be less irascible with my family." Everyday knowing is less simple, perhaps more interesting than epistemic definitions.

So often to "know" means "to be able to". I know how to ski; I know how to play chess or how to prune apple trees. Someone else knows how to surgically remove a tumor. This is not claiming to know how I ski or how I play chess. Simply to know "how to" is to say "I am able to"; not to be able to describe in full detail what is happening when one is doing something. This isn't surprising. Weren't "can" and "know" once the same word? As they still are in German: *kennen*-know and *können*-able-to are scarcely distinguishable in spelling and pronunciation. Doesn't the newborn babe "know" how to suck, though it simply is able to? What are we saying when we affirm that so and so "knows" Shakespeare, or another colleague "knows" Greek, or one neighbor "knows" small motors and another the stock market. Do they possess knowledge that can be set out as so much information? This "know" is subtler than that. It imputes the skill of finding one's way around in a given field; the skill of being able to improvise, to find original answers. After several courses a student might fairly be said still not to "know" Shakespeare. "Know" is a canny word!

Then there is the usage that has biblical sanction and is still common. It recognizes the ability of feelings and intuition, often virtually wordless, to bring us into immediate intimacy with the nature of what we say we know. We say "She new much suffering before she knew happiness." She suffered much before she experienced happiness. To "know" suffering or happiness is to suffer or to be happy. How could we ever come closer to the nature of anything than to be it? And "being it" can still count as knowing in the everyday. All of us "know" our own feelings. We say, so-and-so never "knew" love. As if knowing were access to the secret nature of things. Who can come closer to the nature of wood than the wood sculptor who knows its grains and textures from working with them?

Sometimes we say "I knew all along what the answer was, but didn't realize it." It can't be only me who would say this after a persistent, inarticulate feeling suddenly becomes a simple word clear idea. It's a kind of intuition. In overt situations or in idea exploration feeling can bring us closer to the nature of another person or a new idea than all the words in the dictionaries. The feeling itself must count as agent and content of the knowing.

True to form, the everyday is a happy cluster of ideas about knowing. Not all strictly compatible and yet each justifiably founded in the necessities of its own world.

Knowing and Reality

We use "knowing" as a word of the highest prestige. It marks off a second order of things. It's reserved for settling disputes. To claim one knows raises the degree of certainty to its highest point. Unlike perception, which is personal, variable, and disputable, knowing implicitly claims to be valid for everyone. It rests on the detached objectness of what is known. We believe this without being aware of the enormity of its presumption. It is the most pervasive certainty of all, if seldom brought explicitly to mind: *what* we know must *be;* and be *as* we know it. Knowledge and reality are inseparable thoughts. How could an untruth be knowledge? How could we know something that was nonexistent?

If it is known that two contradictory statements cannot both be true, then that is the reality of the intellectual world. I know water is a compound of hydrogen and oxygen. That is the reality: that is what water is. Even though when I swim in it or glide through it in a canoe I know that water is buoyant, life giving, the presence of a goodness in things that has no chemical formula. And that is reality too. "Knowing" and "reality" are twinned words. To say "I know" is to say "reality". Knowing bows the knee to reality. Reality we think is forever; knowledge is passing.

Action and reality bring another aspect of knowing into view. Readiness to act expresses a confidence in our knowledge of the situation. Action, decision making, presumes an order in the nature of things that will allow our action to make good sense. Of course habit is adequate much of the time. But when it breaks down, knowledge has to take the lead. So, not only knowledge posits the reality of its object, behavior does so too. Can I say that reality is whatever knowledge and behavior must presume in order to be what we believe they are? Can I hold to that and not be subjectivist?

The symbiosis of inner and outer, as a question, dogs me. Is it fully taken up in our everyday sense of knowing? Well, it's clear that knowing is meaningless without a reality to be known. In that sense the inner is inseparable from the outer. But what of the relation of an outer reality to inner knowledge? It is not the same, as I've found out. In the everyday an outer object—the sun in the sky or a minnow in a fish pond—is just exactly what it is in itself quite without any dependence on being known by a human or any other species. End of the symbiosis of inner and outer—in our common thinking. But the question of reality and knowing, of the untouchability of the object of knowledge, of the symbiosis of knower and known, lies outside the normal interests of the everyday. It demands to be studied in its own right. And it challenges to a comparison with the ways other traditions have understood it.

One question has been gradually pushing itself forward: why, and how, do we single out knowing as a relation to the world around us that is unlike any other? We can understand that sense experience, feelings, valuings, help to make the world and reveal it at the same time. Why should knowing be different? From the swarming life of the mind and from the impenetrable thicket of ways we interact with things, how does it happen that knowing is singled out and accorded a special, even the highest, status?

That's the most difficult of historical questions. The Western experience is unlike any other. It records the dominance of the need to find explanations of the way things are. Such was the Greek concern and such has remained the Western concern through modern history. Christianity absorbed the need to revere, to wonder, to hope, leaving the earthy questions to a secular intellect. Only very recently have we begun to squirm uneasily under the bland sovereignty of the detached, theorizing, rational need to explain everything before we can accept it. The intellect, agent of knowing, is unique among human faculties and isolated from the influence of lesser faculties—we have come to believe. This allows us to remove knowing from the symbiosis of inner and outer. After all, philosophical and scientific explanations are not explaining themselves. They must explain what lies outside the process of explanation, or they aren't *explaining* anything.

And so the reality of the object of knowing makes knowing possible and itself is not dependent on being known to be what it is. Thus the gospel. And it's just what must be questioned, in two ways. What guarantees the reality of the intellectual object being explained? It can't be the knowledge we have of it; that would be absurd. Because our knowledge is only our own explanation. If it is to be true, the independent reality of the object and its full nature must be assumed, but on what grounds? Well, we know that from our theory; don't we? No, we don't. We say we know the object, because that is what knowledge is. A perfect circle—and a vicious one. The reality and nature of the object secures the truth of our knowledge; and our knowledge secures the reality and nature of the object! There is no other way to be sure of the reality and nature of things than through knowledge. The symbiosis of inner and outer remains intact, at least on the level of theoretical knowing.

But the way inner and outer maintained themselves in the everyday against the everyday's own understanding of knowing, is just as valid for the sciences and philosophy. Though it will arouse some indignation in those rarefied regions. The reality of the everyday, so I found, is secured by the behavior that must presuppose it. We confer the dignity of reality on whatever our behavior requires to be real if our behavior is to have the sense we want it to have. We can't interact with visions, mirages, floating possibilities and remain sane. At some point reality must enter to anchor the world for us.

If knowing is not a purely semantic connection with objects but always it own kind of behavior and, in degree, always involves some overt interaction with the things one is trying to know, then even philosophic and scientific knowing will presume the reality of what it is trying to know in the very behavior required to know it.

Nagarjuna's long struggle with this question allowed him to see the anomalies of the everyday clearly. I can imagine him asking a student, "Do you know there is a fire blazing in front of you?" "Yes I do." "Good. Now what do you perceive with your senses?" "I see wood in flames, I smell smoke, I feel warmth." "Good. Now where is the 'fire' you knew was blazing in front of you?" "Fire is just what I perceived: flames, smoke, warmth." "But you claimed to 'know' the 'fire'. Do you still think this?" "I see. No, 'fire' is just the name for everything there: wood, flames, smoke, heat." "So I think also," Nagarjuna would have replied.

In my terms, the word "fire" is overlayed on the perceptible phenomena, not merely as a handy word, but as a substantive reality, somehow more real than the burning wood. Fire becomes what we say we know. Our perceptions serve as evidence of its real existence. Such is the power of naming in association with our behavioral need for a world of solid, unchanging realities among which we can, trusting in our knowledge of them, trustingly maneuver.

The same deceptive process—the creation of realities—peoples our world tirelessly with "families", "government", "the economy", "justice", "freedom", "racism", "teenager", forever and ever extending new fields of enterprise obligingly furnished with an encyclopedia of familiar names, each disclosing substantial reality. Two cars collide. The car in front brakes suddenly because of a deer on the edge of the road; the tailgating car, unprepared, buckles both cars so that they need to be towed away. The many versions of what happened interest the police but are not my point. It's the instantaneous use of the word "accident" that makes normal talk possible. Whatever details were observed and can be recounted, and however incompatible they may be with each other, all serve to make known the nature of "the accident". "The accident" is the object that comes to be known. It is the reality behind all the visual reports and retains its reality independent of all the perceptions of all the witnesses. So easily we come to believe that behind any word is an object—independent of our senses and opinions—that must be known.

The everyday is tenacious and has its own reasons. But why is it that vivial exploration can't accept a reality that owes nothing to human experience? Can it be said this way: the distinction the everyday—and science and philosophy—must erect is that between the variable behaviors of knowing—enquiry, curiosity, skepticism, perception, experiment, discussion—and the behaviors of an unquestioning confidence in unchanging realities—"accident", "matter", "field", "light", "relativity", "mind", "intellect", "reason"—confirmed in the bestowal of names. And that this is the enabling basis of cognition?

Plausible? For most it will seem too much. But it permits a

blunt observation. The reality and nature of a known something is not given to us except in our knowing it. That behavioral attitudes and procedures are always part of knowing is a vivial emphasis, but the thought is meant to hold for any view of knowledge. It's not just that the object of our knowing can't be allowed an existence independent of our knowing. This was Nietzsche's point when he argued that we would require a second means of access to a known object if we were to be able to test our knowledge of it. And Wittgenstein's point: we can describe an object only in exactly the same language we use to describe our knowledge of it. Vivial exploration gives the matter a different emphasis. What if our sense of reality derives from the necessity of behavior, whether knowing behavior or some other, to understand itself as interacting with realities that justify the behavior? Would one not be simply insane if one went through the motions of interacting with things one didn't believe were there? Either way, the object is raised above the details of discussion—mysterious as this is—and is treated as an element in an order of reality lying beyond the behavior and processes of coming to know it.

If we can say this of automobile accidents, why not of laboratory knowledge and philosophical and religious knowledge? None of these will be able to be sure of the reality of its chosen objects—natural laws, self-evident first principles, omnipotent deities—apart from the behavior required to come to know them.

Well, that's a first look at the ways and worth of knowing. Knowing is the heartbeat of the everyday, and of all behavior. Confidence in knowing imbeds human existence in a foundation of reality. Knowing has meaning only if and as it secures us a hold on reality. There seem to be three mighty articles of faith in our twentieth century Western uses of the word "knowing". Knowing brings us closer to the nature of things than any other type of experience; it is our way of becoming intimate with the world around us. Knowing is a singular relationship to things, an imperceptible, unique bond between the knowing intellect and what it knows, a bond that cannot be reduced to anything less than itself. Knowing guarantees the reality of its object even as real objects guarantee the possibility of knowing.

These articles of faith hold for the everyday, if implicit, and for philosophy and science. But they are not a mere academic definition. They have a hold on our life sense like a profound fairy tale. It's a core theme of the human drama. Yet, we have no way of knowing that this notion of knowing is itself an instance of knowing. Knowing cannot itself be made into an object of knowing. If this is sound, then we appear to be flying on the wings of natural belief. Knowledge can't be the bedrock of human existence, however much the belief that it is enables us to live. Of course we don't believe that knowledge is our only way of staying in touch with the world around us, but it is our belief that in matters of importance we always have knowledge as the ultimate touchstone of decision.

The Family of Knowing

Not too fast. Our everyday is no more than the everyday of North American English at the end of the twentieth Christian century. And our philosophy and science are unique to the Greek-European tradition. How many other everydays and philosophies have there been—and are! Yet the problems of knowing are at the heart of all classical thought traditions. That our plain word "know" belongs to one of the most ancient of human families makes this clear. *Jnā* is what the peoples said who flowed into India from Asia 3,000 or 4,000 years ago. *Gnosis* it became in Greece; *cognoscere,* in Rome; *Kennen,* in German; and "know" in English. And that *jnā*'s older brother *vid, veda,* telling more the possession of knowledge, made much the same migration strengthens the family ties. Greek had it as *oida*—Plato's *eidos,* the object of true knowledge; Latin as *videre* to see; German as *Wissen,* knowledge possessed and available; and English has kept it in "wit", "wise", "wisdom". The persistence of these words through millenia and many languages marks the problem as more than a modern Western specialty. Can we decline to learn from the others?

What fascinating questions *jnā* brings with it wherever it is used in Sanskrit. The Upanishads pivot on its broad power. The passages in the Great Forest Upanishad where Yajnavalkya speaks teach me the most: "He who knows Truth becomes Truth". What a startling use of the word "know". He doesn't say, as we might, "He who would know the laws of the universe must first shed his private interests." Our knowing is proud of the distinction between the knower and the scientific laws he or she knows. In Sanskrit the highest knowing dissolves that distinction. Knower and known become one. That the Buddhist emphasized the importance of knowing in a negative way still makes it central: it is ignorance to believe that truth can be found so long as the individual is separated from the way of things by a belief in knowledge.

The way that dangerous heresy of late European antiquity, gnosticism, used the Greek word *gnosis,* knowledge, was almost sanskritic. For the one part meaning their own special set of truths: that God was pure light, that each individual had a spark of this light in his or her spirit and that the destiny of the individual was to become one with the divine light. And then their belief that *gnosis* was the happening of this reunion with god. What scope for the problem of knowledge!

And the Taoists from classical China. Strange they are and yet appealing. Their grave and humorous conversations on knowledge treat it as a vain striving fed by ignorance. Not unlike the Buddhists. Their distinction between the "little" and the "great" understanding is especially relevant. It puts the world of individual interests and the everyday talk it conjures into existence under the "little" understanding. Then the "great" understanding is free to become the wordless awareness of the nature of things: their unquenchable spontaneity for ever and ever. Which is the human way of becoming one with the way of all things. Taoists would have thought our science an almost willful attempt to estrange humans from the world they live in.

Friedrich Nietzsche's ferocious attacks on the modern Western idea of knowledge are strongly compatible with Taoist thought, though hardly as gracious. For both—as for Upanishadic thinkers, Buddhists, and Gnostics—the enterprise of systematic cognition erects the world into a self-contained object standing over against the one trying to know. This denigrates both the would-be knower and the world, and blocks an understanding of either. Heavy weather, but so I read them.

Nietzsche is a paradox. His attacks on the presumption of knowledge—seeing knowledge as linguistic illusion, as will to power, as a subspecies of error, as not the arbiter of human destiny—are directed solely at the European tradition. Yet he has done more to make it possible for European thinkers to understand classical Chinese and Indian thought than scholars in these fields themselves have been able to do so. And no one has taken his measure. Our scientists persist in denaturing nature by their laboratory procedures. Our philosophers persist in declining to admit the Greek dream has ended. Nietzsche is the primal renegade, the strongest voice yet in what is already the struggle of the next century. Science will have to fight to retain its power as the universal church. What forces will array themselves in this struggle isn't clear yet. But in Nietzsche's shadow who can forget that life is greater than our theories of it?

No doubt though, our knowing is a member of an ancient family of the grandest aspirations. But how disparate its members! What makes them a family? What unaware aspirations do they share? What do Vedic *Brahman,* Taoist Way, Gnostic pure light have in common with Greek and European philosophic and scientific truth?

Their most striking common belief is that they can approach the seat and abode of what they are most certain of—human fate within the whole of things—only through use of the word *knowledge* in one of its family variants. The Taoist Way is silent, and so takes up all things into one harmony beyond verbal cognition. True, Gnostic and Vedic thinking preserve the word for knowing into and through their resolutions of the human predicament. But they alter its use and significance beyond recognition. Fascinating. What power their words for knowing retain even in their transformation! Vedic thinkers could say that *Brahman* (Being, Truth) is "known"; this, even though it becomes one with the individual "knower". We would say this makes it unknowable. And the Gnostic god is "known" in an experience in which the knowing individual human ceases to exist. Both attempting to express the ultimate in intimacy.

No reconciling these different understandings of knowing. But somehow they are of one family. How much that tells me. Knowing carries the furthest aspirations of its devotees. Whatever experiences these come to rest in, they are understood, positively or negatively, in terms of knowing. Those who hold to the word—Vedic thinkers, Gnostics, modern scientists—give it the significance of ultimate certainty. An apotheosis of everyday belief.

Knowing is their grandest metaphor. And from all there is so much to be learned.

Knowing and Behavior

The everyday showed that we don't treat knowing as an isolated function. We must perform many acts—inner and outer—many times before we understand the worth of what we're doing. What we know is what we do—writing, thinking, feeling being included—turned inside out. The family of great knowers will have something to say about that. Of course they had no need to ask precisely my question. Still . . .

The passage in Plato's Republic that sets out the training and achievements of those Plato would admit into his advanced classes is eloquent. He saw the strongest interdependence between the nature of the student and what he will become capable of knowing. To learn what Plato believed a philosopher should know, the student must be born with a love for the kind of knowledge that reveals the essence of things; he must be capable of apprehending the eternal. Plato is quite blunt. Anyone who is to be capable of grasping his truth must have a certain "paradigm" in his soul, a certain conformation of characteristics. He is to be just and gentle, should love truth and hate falsehood, should be indifferent to bodily pleasures, have no fear of death, be endowed with measure and grace, be readily guided to the ideal reality of things. Our graduate schools aren't quite so selective! And Plato adds that one becomes like what one knows: the idea of the good. As this is not known conceptually as all other ideas are, but in a whole vision, he would have some sympathy with my question.

That the interpreters of the Sanskrit Vedas should have adopted the same stance toward their pupils as Plato to his must be of some importance. Shankara's treatment of this question in his commentary on the *Brahma Sūtras* is uncannily parallel to Plato's. He insists on the student's ability to discriminate between the perishable and the imperishable, on the renunciation of personal reward as the fruit of action, both here and in the hereafter. He expects control of one's bodily organs, control of one's senses, and control of one's mind. And the key: the student must have a longing for liberation from his confining finite self.

This statement of the behavioral prerequisites to the study of the truth of things is, put my way, a description of the truth to be arrived at, turned out in the idiom of behavior. To discriminate the true nature of the imperishable and the perishable posits the Vedantic belief that the eternal is accessible to human experience. To renounce the fruit of actions is a turning away from the perishability of everyday things, as is the control of the senses. Both teach the worthlessness of perishable things. Control of the mind—meditation—secures this turning away from the perishable everyday and offers a way of discovering and conforming to the imperishable. In short, the behavior Plato and Shankara enjoin implicitly anticipates the truth to be discovered, and this, in turn, becomes the pervasive sense of what the student is doing.

The classical Taoists are so close to what I want to say, I wonder if I'm plagiarizing them! Both the Lao Tzu and Chuang Tzu texts replace knowing with a certain behavior. It's not, as with Plato and Shankara, that suitable behavior is prerequisite to the culminating insight. The Taoists have no insight into the way of things other than to behave in harmony with it. And I realized that only recently! It's not just Chuang Tzu's bombshell: "There must be a true man before there is true knowledge." It's more that the behavior of a true man can be described only in exactly the same words, given exactly the same attributes, as the Great Way itself—and vice versa. Both are without personal purpose, for both there is no finality in the concerns and prejudices and talk of the everyday, both are at home in wordless silence, both are self-directed. Chuang Tzu reaches the limit of emphasis when he says he wants to smash up his body, drive out his senses and intellect, do away with understanding, and make himself one with the Great Way. Lao Tzu, a little less dramatic, wishes to create without possession, to nurture things without ruling them, to master all things through clarity and innocence without the need to act. It is as though the Way can show itself only in the behavior of wise persons. As if the function of the wise were to mirror and reveal the subtleties of the Way. The only other classical thinkers who interweave thought and behavior so completely must be Middle Way Buddhists. They have no way of describing the Buddha's Way except to point to the enlightened person who is walking it; and no way of describing the enlightened person except to say he or she is on the Buddha's Middle Way.

Nietzsche might wish to offer himself as a witness at this point. He would certainly be an eager witness, but a somewhat ambivalent one. He does try to destroy knowledge by showing it the plaything of mostly unaware life forces and feelings, but he does not credit the intellect with a reciprocal influence on them. And I can't accept that. Certainly his dionysian exhortation to live "yeah" to all things is the behavioral analogue to his theoretical insight that all things are dipped in the well of eternity, and so of equal value. And certainly his dictum, "The germ of every philosophy lies in the moral belief of its author", implies that reason gives expression to behavioral values. His "will to power" and the "superhuman" are summons to action, implying behavior appropriate to them. Even the eternal return of all things, though often set out as a theory, is a way of accepting ourselves and is a behavioral test to select those capable of surviving in the future.

It's the absence of emphasis on the reverse dependence—the dependence of behavior on the clarifying and driving force of ideas—that is disturbing. Surely he overplays his hand when he says that our morals are like bubbles on the stream of our instincts, and only that. Value sense can let us know what our instincts are telling us and can influence the forms they take. But Nietzsche, thunderstorm over Europe that he was and has increasingly become, could not complete a revolution by himself. There is a gap in his thought. He was never quite clear that his own theories, if advanced as true, contradicted his own life's work, which was to put an end to philosophical truth. His own theory of the importance of instinct and feeling in the formation of "truth" could be, according to this very theory, no more than an expression of his own instincts and feelings. But not true. He sometimes forgot that the worth of his theories was not to be true, but was their power to arouse the kinds of behavior he thought would save the human species.

The American pragmatists are close by at this point. I couldn't be a pragmatist, accusations to the contrary. My early enthusiasm for William James didn't survive his determination to give metaphysics a worthy place among her "sister sciences". And Dewey's obsession with experimental science at the model of all knowing seemed suffocatingly narrow. Still, many of Dewey's formulations were promising. Knowing is itself a kind of action, he could say, the only kind that securely clothes existence with meanings. Or, ideas are not a picture of what exists independent of them, but of acts to be performed. Or, ideas are plans of operations to be performed. This is so promising. Why am I not a pragmatist?

A pervasive, uncritical American naturalism fueled the interests of Dewey and that cloyed. He seemed oblivious to any human possibilities not encompassed in social and physical science. His enthusiasm for useful "instrumentalities" made him a kind of technocrat. His concept of behavior relevant to knowing included only such overt acts as can be reduced to an exact methodology. He was obsessed by prescriptions for controlled social research and the determination of social good by planned experiment. So, even though the pragmatists saw clearly, as Plato and Nietzsche and the Taoists and the Vedic thinkers did, that thought and behavior are inseparable, that thought is a kind of behavior and behavior, a kind of thinking, we are nonetheless alien. Dewey became virtually a philosopher of science. Not a favorable base for anyone who wants to set Western science in the panorama of all human attempts to understand the worth and limits of knowledge.

Western Science and Other Traditions

And what else should our interest be at this time but to attempt just that? We are so deep in the habit of believing knowledge to be objective, independent of feelings and universally valid, that we have forgotten this is merely one point of view. We have accepted the consequence, equally unawarely, that only that aspect of our world which can be so known is important, indeed, as some would have it, only what can be so known, exists. We are the first human beings who have conceived knowledge so narrowly that, far from opening up our world to unknowable wonders, it confines us, soul and mind, to the rock-bound prison of physical science.

But our science is not in every sense unique. Recollections of other classical ways of knowing can allow us to see that Western science is itself a classical instance of knowing. As in the older traditions, our science too understands the highest, most testable, most useful knowing to be a close interweave of behavior and comprehension. Never mind the differences between Taoist or Buddhist "behavior" and scientific laboratory techniques. The strong axis of learned behavior runs through them all. John Dewey saw this forcefully for his own time but didn't seem aware of the range of its historical validity.

And yet, the differences between our knowing and the older ways! The Platonist, the Vedic poet, the Buddhist, the Taoist, and Nietzsche, too, opened out the fields of behavior that could integrate with knowledge to the furthest reaches of human experience. No less. The intellect was not left free to think what it might please to. Most of these thinkers didn't believe humans possessed an autonomous faculty of knowing in any case. Such a belief was reserved for Aristotelians and their modern European reincarnations: Descartes, Leibnitz, Newton, and the others. What courage Plato and the Sanskrit and Chinese thinkers showed in trusting to the stability and clarity of human experience as they did. There was no meaning to their knowledge if it were not of such surety and self-evidence that anyone, with suitable guidance, could attain it and test it in his or her own experience; even in experience that questioned the very destiny of human beings. Knowing, or its transformed equivalent, could be as embracing as life itself, because the behavior with which it was integrated was itself so embracing.

There is one way Western science differs from this. But it is a way that sets it universes apart. We restrain knowing to a passage as narrow as the straits between Scylla and Charibdis. The behavior we recognize as most essential to knowing is the skilled, technical handling of laboratory machines. Manipulating such machines for the purpose of eliciting information about physical processes and the mathematical procedures required to interpret the information so elicited are believed to be the behavior indispensable to testing and yielding knowledge. Devising intermediate "models" of nature and deducing subprinciples needed to "bridge" data to them certainly belongs to approved scientific behavior. As does dedication to exactness. And everyone agrees that individual gifts of imagination and inventive power are essential to effective laboratory work. So, as in all the classical examples, what can be said to be known is strictly dependent on the behavior by and in which the knowledge is attained.

That is much to have in common, but there it ends. What they do not have in common has the profoundest effect on their views of the world and of human destiny in it. The older thinkers believed there was nothing in human experience, even in its furthest, most frightening reaches, that they could not accept as matter for assimilating and testing in their disciplines of behavior and so accept as something they might know. The reality they required themselves to live with was as open as human imagination itself.

Western science is a kind of knowing that implies a radically narrower and simpler notion of reality. It accepts as knowable only that aspect of the world that its laboratory machines can detect and report on. Rational explanations of the data may count as knowledge. Of course the scientist may believe in the reality of other worlds not accessible to laboratory experiments. The Christianity of Isaac Newton! But the overpowering fact remains: with the dominance of the physical sciences in Europe and America a world-view has emerged that declines to accept as real anything outside the range of these sciences. A powerful, if imprecise, naturalism has seized hold of our minds. Today one must virtually apologize for introducing anything as real that is not scientifically established. Our science of the past 400 years is inextricably one with the prevalent world-view: the origin and termination of the physical universe set the horizons of human knowledge and the reality we live in.

Harsh words. And yet my lasting sense of what is going on in our time. The science believers most often turn on me with the objection, "But our science is rational. Appeal to sentiment or belief or value preference is rigidly suppressed. The older schools you mention are not critical as we are, they accept verdicts other than those of the intellect. They do not qualify as knowers, not in our sense. After all, only science is scientific." Well and loyally spoken.

It's true that Vedantists, Taoists, Buddhists, Nietzsche, though they are tireless and gifted reasoners, do not claim that what they know has been secured for them by their intellects, nor would they want to. Intellect is not for them the highest human faculty, as most of us believe we believe. Each of the classical views is grounded in a powerful sense of the way it is with life. This is the base of their explicit ideas, but is not related to them by proof.

The confident way Taoists presume that heaven and earth and all the beings in and on them are within one universe of meaning astounds one of our time. That individual and political behavior, the behaviors of poet and sage are all comprehended within the laws of nature; that the course of life and death is one rhythm binding heaven and earth; that not only are all things within one complex harmony, but that there is an eternal reality sustaining the harmony; and that the hidden and strange ways of heaven and earth can be discovered in peaceful and silent contemplation. All this is heart and core of Taoism. Yet none of it is secured by scientific procedures. It is their sense of the way of things. One just has to live that way to confirm it.

And it's no different with Buddhism. How dare Buddha pronounce his "attainment of the deathless" without offering a single sentence in proof? Or tell his tiny circle of fellow strivers that anyone can do the same if he or she will just test his claim? Where does his certainty come from? I say, again, from a sense of the way of life lying so deep in himself and his time that it made the vivial demand for the imperishable at once self-evident and unaware. Everything is perishable—except the imperishable. Every living being, including the human, is born and reborn endlessly until it can free itself from the ignorant acceptance of the perishable world as reality and from naive trust in the supremacy of the senses and the mind. Until it has attained the plane of the imperishable.

"But these are just ancient religious movements. We are talking about modern scientific knowledge." Not quite so. But for the moment, what about Nietzsche? At least he's not ancient, nor a model of modern theory of knowledge either. He couldn't be. He's more a theorist of nonknowledge, and more than a theorist. He argues for his ideas with the vehemence and self-confidence of a prophet. And with prophetic indifference to rational proof. In the nineteenth century.

Where did he come from? In his Lutheran pastoral home he would have learned to see the truths of the world as traps for the unwary. He would have learned the truth was of another order, concealed from the secular eye. His years as a student of Greek and Latin gave him proof that life need not be as nihilistic as he found it in nineteenth century Europe. A ruthless smashing of the idols of European culture was his only way of breaking out of the falsity and smugness of the everyday, for which he saw his own Christianity responsible. He needed a larger and freer human form than he found in his world. I do believe Nietzsche quested all his life for an original salvation. His notion that all things had been baptized in the well of eternity and therefore, if only one peeled away conventional coverings, were of equal worth was profoundly disruptive of European religious, scientific and class values. That his intent was not philosophical but vivial is clear from his striking thought: it is not enough to *say* I accept all things as eternal; I must also *live* them as eternal. This isn't rational theory; it's a kind of behavior: a way out of European nihilism.

Knowing and Rationality

"Yes, yes," I hear my laboratory friends saying, "but that is all religious or ethical or existential." Of course such thinkers are carried by unexamined belief systems, but the kind of knowing developed in the modern West is not like Taoism, Buddhism, Plato, or Nietzsche. It is rational, testable, and free of unprovable superstitions. It is different. It is unique."

Well, yes, it is unique—that's obvious. But how unique? Its precise knowing behavior is unique; its narrow focus on physical nature is unique. But is it unique in being free of unaware presumptions?

If it were, we would have to be of a different species than knowers of other times and cultures. Because they turned out to have been borne by a sense of life that, though not prescribing specific answers, did determine of what kind they would be and within what range they would lie. Their presumption was that our minds are integrated with all of us in a way that makes reasoning without presumptions impossible.

This is an enveloping problem. Didn't Descartes assume, on religious grounds, a benevolent deity willing that the world conform to the requirements of science? Didn't he assume he was a member of a superior species, inhabiting a world for which he had no responsibility—except to know it as far as possible? Didn't

Newton study space and motion and light and calculus as if these were lifeless objects? And regard himself as in the service of his god? And don't contemporary scientists, most noticeably physicists, treat all elements of the physical universe as so many given accidents?

Now these are not scientific attitudes, growing in the scientist's mind without roots or nourishment from outside science. Behind scientific objectivity and the sole importance of physical objects is the largely unaware assumption that the human being, though living in the physical world, is not of it. It is matter and the human is intellect. One need feel no other interest in the objects of one's research than to know them. Their being and fate is not the scientist's responsibility—except for the paradox, a paradox we can be grateful for, that some bioscientists are concerned about the life forms they study. Still, we are so immersed in the soulless physicality of the universe that we forget how nearly unique this belief is. Each of the other kinds of knowing I'm familiar with thought the one knowing was of the same essence as what he or she knew. The human was not isolated in an indifferent universe as the scientist and most of us today are. So, our science lives off presumptions even as the other ways of knowing did.

It is unique in believing that the intellect is the primary bond between humans and the things in their world. Buddhists, Vedantists, and Taoists thought of human situations not as factual, but as opportunities for the enlightened return to the truth of things. Nietzsche wanted Dionysian action to be the bond. Our contemporary faith in scientific truth has burgeoned into a secular church as religious faith has retired into itself and left the field open. The scientific isolation of intellect is not rational. It is a profound habit of thinking, a faith, nothing more. Yet knowing is believed to give us the world as it is in itself. We quite literally see the world as the laws and data of science turned inside out for our easy viewing. The "nature of things" is as described by the physical sciences and by them alone.

In short, quite like the other members of the knowing family, our science is not free of a deep cluster of beliefs that determine what it will accept *as* knowing. Why should it be? Are we of another species? Have we discovered a science that establishes the claims of science? The long pointing shadow of inner-outer falls across the page here. Why should, how could, the world our scientist knows be any more independent of the scientist than the world of other kinds of knowers was independent of them? The problem of knowledge is the most severe test of the inseparability of inner and outer. The specific genius of Western scientists is no ground for believing they are above the laws of knowing.

This doesn't invalidate science. It allows it to be more human. Even if there were an autonomous faculty of reason in humans it would not be an appropriate means of discovering a world in which humans must live and find their own worth. We're compound of inherited powers and ignorances, of acquired habits, spontaneous feelings, and an unaccountable life sense. How can, why should, reason alone speak for all that? We're not of a rational substance.

The science enthusiasts will insist that large sectors of their work is nonetheless rational, that science should not be grouped with ideologies or semireligious societies that follow one leader and secure their convictions not by reasoning, but by behavior discipline and rituals. Science, they will insist, is not like that.

And I will insist that it is—if we look carefully enough. "Rationality" is itself a cult word. It is useful only in the safe harbors of logic and mathematics and becomes a matter of silent, perhaps unaware, prayer when it puts out onto the high seas. Because it is a faith, rationality is powerless to find rational grounds for itself. Humans are powerless to uncover the first principles of all things; that is, principles so primary they stand alone in the self-evident light of their own truth. This is so in all fields. Clarity and conviction come not from one founding rational principle, but from a weave of many principles and beliefs, not all compatible with one another. As the behaviors of knowing progress, one principle tends to emerge and establish its dominance. The more a belief can explain, the more self-evident it appears to be. In part based on lesser beliefs that sink into forgottenness. The kind of sense one is looking for in things will determine which belief becomes self-evident. To say this is not to belittle science, but to include it in the great family of knowing.

Western science is a heroic effort to make a reality out of the impenetrable world humans find themselves struggling to come to vivial terms with. It's worthy to take its place among the other heroic struggles to know. But we mustn't let it limit our understanding of the many ways there are of knowing. Our science is more peripheral to human life than earlier classical ways of knowing were. Its narrow focus allows the physical universe to swell into inappropriate importance in our thinking: witness our popular cosmologies. It is the question of our time: will this hold on the public mind exhaust itself before it has irremediably crippled our ability to understand the world as the home of human beings and not merely as a colossal physical accident?

Knowing in Our Time

Our science is the only kind of knowing that begins by seeing the world as a vast expanse of objects each behaving in obedience to the laws of its physical nature. Not as the meaningful countenance and gesture of a superhuman natural power, but utterly dead to human values. This brings a special interest, purpose, and stance with it. Doesn't the scientist have to feel set over against the world, distanced from it, unique in his or her power to make all of creation into the object of study? What the church abandoned, science conquered. The resulting struggle between science and religion was inevitable. It's the most striking feature of the modern West, and the root cause of our science becoming inhuman and religion peripheral. What would a classical Greek or Chinese or Indian or a medieval Christian say about the worth of a way of knowing that sets the human person to one side, retaining only abstract reasoning power, that interposes intricate machines between the world and the abstract human knower, and that refuses the dignity of knowledge to anything that is not data from those machines?

Harsh thoughts. But it's a shock to realize that our only sanctified way of knowing bans so much of human power and intelligence from its observance. Why should space and time—masks of vivial worth—set the bounds to what we need to know, to what we can know, to what we are allowed to know? Is this indifference to the human spirit history's revenge for centuries of religious indifference to the body? The only writers these days who dare speculate about the universe as a whole are theoretical physicists, whose quaint metaphors of big bangs and black holes sound like a story from another world.

It is widely held that such theories hold up the frame within which we must now view ourselves and the destiny of the human world. Nonsense, I say. We are in a nihilistic time, understandably. We are emerging from a profound Christian culture. But our cosmologies reduce nihilism to barren and brutal pictures. Science is not the cause of nihilism, but its most seductive voice. Science is a vivial parable telling of our loss of sense and meaning in human life.

And of course it's more than that. The public mind has embraced science as the source of truth and accorded it the status of an established church. No ancient priest ever uttered more mysterious, more powerful words than the formula $E = mc^2$. No ancient religion had more devoted acolytes than our sciences have in their white-robed laboratory researchers. "Science" is our synonym for fact, truth, knowledge. It gives us our sense of reality. And it infuses our public thinking with a paradigm of democratic behavior: sober, secular, honest, collective, according equality to all—facts. "Science" tells the public mind more about itself and about the nature of humans and more about realistic purposes and acceptable values than any other word in currency today. It persuades us that only science can save our dying planet. It doesn't often tell us that our science is the first kind of knowledge we know of that has directly caused the deterioration of the human habitat.

Sounds inflated. But it's got to be so. Still, where does our science stand as a kind of knowing? Does it know anything? Does it tell us the truth of things? In the plain sense the answer would have to be no. That sounds maliciously perverse. But it isn't, because I would give the same answer if the question were asked of Plato's theories, or Taoist or Buddhist thought, or Vedanta or Nietzsche. Science doesn't give us truth, because humans have no access to truth . . . , not being gods.

Science deals as little in truth as philosophy or theology or history. Of course the physical sciences have an array of theories, principles, and models and a vast range of "observations" from their laboratory apparatuses. We're so used to this we forget that every observation becomes data or fact only when it fits a theory. Atomic physicists are explicit about this. Electrons and protons can't be given precise characteristics until the scientist intervenes with a choice of paradigm: wave or particle. This is a perfect example of the inseparability of inner and outer. And of the importance of behavior in the emergence of knowledge. No part of nature enters a science laboratory except as an answer to a question that is important to humans. The scientist knows something only about the adequacy of a theory to make sense of data, not about the way nature is in itself. It's more precise to speak of the validation of a theory than of its truth.

Because we can never know if a theory is true or not. But we can be sure whether it enables us to foresee some events accurately enough to allow us to interact effectively with them. What science knows is confined within the limits of its own behavior with its machines and within the limits of the adequacy of its own theories. So described our science shares a basic character with older kinds of knowing.

Like them it receives its impulse not so much from a detached scientific curiosity as from a need to explore the sources from which we may understand the way of all things. Most scientists will be impelled by the need to penetrate more deeply into the mysteries of a cosmos governed by mathematical laws whose beauty are open to ever-fresh discovery. Even if they turn out to be the laws of chaos. Knowledge—religious or scientific or philosophical—confers the power, and the right, to share in the governance of one's world.

But one characteristic science does not share with the others: science is the knowing permitted by a given technology. Not by a given technique—all knowing rests in techniques, if unawarely. Our science must ask questions and interpret answers only as its machines can fit these to nature. This makes the worth of technology the seminal question for us. The human mind always inclines to assume the form of the machines it serves. It's commonplace today to be told that the human brain is a piece of high technology! And that soon we'll be able to manufacture computers that have a consciousness like our own! One must wonder: what will break the spell nuclear-electronic technology has cast over us?

Nevertheless, science confirms what other ways of knowing had made clear: knowing is not the activity of an isolated intellect, but is its own kind of behavior, inseparable from inner habits of valuing and overt interaction with the world one is said to know.

That the prescribed kind of knowing behavior differs with each vision of the cosmos and every expression of its truth is clear. And as it should be.

Knowing and Person

So, that's the course, for me. Knowing is not the privileged function of an upper-class faculty. It's the achievement of nothing less than a full person—body, feelings, imagination, thought. We will know the world only as we can live it within the limitations of human senses, feelings, mind, imagination, and will. Any knowledge we have of the world will be an essentially behavioral exploration of it. What humans know about will be a human world. Not of course only about humans. There will always be gods and demons, other living beings, and nature's power and beauty. This leaves out many metaphysical niceties, but if Buddha's *nirvāṇa* and the Taoist's Great Way are, in my sense, within the human world, metaphysics can bide its time.

From the Vedas and Plato to Western theoretical physics I can now see a central core in the ways people have understood what they are saying when they take the great word "knowing" in their mouths. They reserve the word for the moment when their search for sense comes to rest in a natural fulfillment. This is not at the end of a *cul de sac,* but the moment of greatest freedom: at the moment when no further behavioral discoveries appear to be possible. Freedom is the limit and the fullness of one's behavioral possibilities. The world so discovered is crowned with the title "reality" or "being". Kant must have believed he had penetrated to the brink of human possibilities when he realized that the existence of God is secured by the freedom of a human person. And Nietzsche must have felt the same when he realized he had to live the eternal return to make it true.

Every theory about the way things are—from the doglike cynicism of Diogenes to the idealism of Immanuel Kant—presupposes its author's approval of the behavior that enables its discovery, that secures it, and that makes the teaching of it possible. The theory doesn't evoke the behavior, nor does the behavior inspire the theory: neither causes the other. Behavior and knowledge are inseparable. Behavior has to find its ultimate sense in the knowing it enables, and knowing, its strength from the vivial worth of the behavior that secures it. As we are so will we know. The bounds set to our inner behavior as persons are the bounds of our knowing.

PERSON

Our Person

Knowing knowing has been crucial—that's for sure. It drew a stronger behavioral significance out of the explorations of inner and outer, space, time, and words. And would do the same for what ever aspect of the everyday was explored: freedom, gender, nature, democracy, technology, . . . Each would open up, not verbal truths, but the life sense hidden in them. While leaving the rules of Western epistemology by the wayside.

But now, what to do with the masks of reality and the hand of fingers outstretched into the boundless life they obscured? What holds them together? They can't be meaningless. Because they aren't. The way we live with them allows them to cohere meaningfully. Knowing knowing said it is possible for the worth of all things, so far as experienced in freedom, to cohere in a sense of the way of life itself.

For a person, so it turned out. Why person? How did that word slip into my speech? Habit? The protean genius of language? Or simply that "person" has recently and swiftly taken over our thinking about the human individual? In any case it has become our most favored and esteemed word for the human being. It hasn't always been so; and it's not so today in all languages. But in English it marks the importance of the individual as the new center of the cosmos. Gods and demons have faded and left person as our latest deity. The word works magic. It tells us of the radical equality of all human beings. Sex does not affect the validity of person, nor race, nor religion, nor class, nor intelligence; person has become our quintessential human being. A person is a self-starting, self-directing, self-responsible, "creative", potentially perfect being. Who needs another god?

Persuasive talk. But what becomes of person in the marketplace of our public world? We face an explosive contradiction. Dominant technological and political forces, not wholly different, have seized on person as consumer and voter and so turned the notion against itself. Democracy in a society of picture rhetoric rubs out the "creative" individual. That we want a human to be a mini-cosmos of all values and then suffocate him or her into a docile recipient of machine toys, machine pictures, machine ideas, and machine politics is our paradox and our challenge and our tragedy. Person has become the meeting ground of a powerful individual and a faceless cipher. We have been anesthetized for service in a society that has no place for individuals who are radically themselves. Isn't each of us as public person, as citizen participant in the television fairy tale of our public life, a faceless mirror image of an impersonal science, an inhuman technology, an ubiquitous cash nexus and tribal politics? Isn't the ambition to become a "balanced psyche" sucking at our own life forces in a kind of closed circuit? What were once superhuman powers are now denied a divine origin, and the person has become their heir.

Yes. That's our very conundrum: both are true! We are living out the most fateful clash of vivial forces our history has known. The ancient wisdom that took the person as being, in essence, more than merely human is still alive among us. Alive enough—we've got to hope—to survive until it can again become real, even though masked over by the forces of scientific naturalism, for now. To survive it will have to be rediscovered, as simply as possible, in new ways. Our own ways.

That's quite a rush of my own enthralments! But what can one feel more strongly about? I will stand, or fall, by one simple conviction: person is now our flagship and our colors. How else than through recapturing the horizons of human powers— a fresh concept of person—can we establish a base for free and ample thought again sometime in the future? It won't be a reenactment of philosophy or Christianity, nor of Taoism, Buddhism, or Vedanta. If naturalistic science and power technology ever become our sacred book of wisdom—as yet they are merely the habits of the public person, unconsecrated—the human adventure would be at its end.

Possible Persons for Vivial Exploration

But back to the question. If the term "person" speaks our highest regard for the human individual, what could it say of interest to vivial exploration? What *is* the essential nature of a human being? Is it to be the member of the animal world with the largest brain, the temporarily dominant species? Or a being open to physiological exploration, definition, and understanding? Or a being with a psychic nature not wholly independent of its body, but still functioning according to its own laws? Or a being unique for its gift of an intellect capable of reducing the processes of nature to precise laws in its freedom of self-determination? Or a being of spiritual origins cut off from its source and godhead so long as it exists in a body, but capable of returning to its original home?

The field is rich—with theories—which I can't use. The old question must be asked again: how do I begin? Where pick up the thread of sense that winds its way to person? The notion is so fragmented. Body is a strong focus; physiology is in the ascendant; so is the psyche and its maladies, the theoretical intellect, the free will, person as social artifact. So the fragments and their theories, but neither offers a starting point. It's our nearest, most immediate experience that resonates person.

Many would say, body. All right, but which body? "The" body or "my" body? We do function it's true as social beings primarily through our physical presence and behavior. But is the body itself a primary experience? We can't experience anything without it, but isn't' its singular importance a gradual discovery, indeed something of a theoretical construct? Those boyhood foot races, wrestling in the snow, headstanding, were not body experiences. They were inner joy. And the nausea from whirling around on the piano stool was just as inner. My body wasn't sick. I was. The body as such wasn't there. Is it much before the early teen years that one learns to single out one's own body as my *body,* not just me, from the other physical objects around one? Won't it be clear, even to a body thinker, that one's own body is a sophisticated idea, not a simple given?

Mind? Start with sense impressions and inner perceptions that empiricists believe are the original elements of consciousness? Basic and importunate they are; but all living beings exist by feelings and sensations. The tiniest worm shrinks from an electric shock and wiggles toward a morsel of food. In any case the innocent primacy of sensations and feelings is a theory, not an experience. Only a rugged empiricist believes there is raw material in the mind. Sensations become what they are for us only after we form them into a world of objects and causes and crown them with names. Of course I'm no friend of empiricism, but what in raw sensation would open up a way into the puzzles of person?

Spirit? Could we seek Plato's soul-psyche? Christian idealists are sure of this. All individual beings have bodies and sensations; and most, in degree, have some calculating ability that in humans is called reason. But only the human individual has a moral conscience and a soul that joins one with the secrets of divinity. Whatever makes humans immortal is what makes them persons is the thought.

And great names are behind this thought. It can't be ignored as a concept of person, but is it a first opening into an exploration of person? Whether Plato or St. Paul or Augustine or Immanuel Kant tells us this, none of them would hold that the immortal soul itself is indubitably give in our experience. That Plato and Kant each needed an intricate pattern of concepts to make this idea tenable in conscience tells me that the spiritual person does not present itself identifiably in our experience. Plato had to divide the world into visible and invisible realms before he could support the idea of an individual soul-psyche, immortal. Kant had to distinguish between the world of science and a suprasensible world to make the spiritual person plausible. Their very labors tell that the soul doesn't obligingly announce itself in our experience. Of course St. Paul and Augustine needed no such philosophical scaffolding. Passionate belief in the Christian truth took its place. But even they do not establish the spirit-person as a fact of experience. That humans are spiritual beings is an inarguable conclusion—if you start from an inarguable presumption of god's existence. It's a mighty conclusion. It may even be tenable. But it isn't a given in everyone's experience from which vivial exploration could take its beginning.

Is anything so given? There *is* something, and it's an ancient thought. If we ask any human individual, "How do you understand yourself as a human being? What makes you sure you are a person?" The answer will almost certainly be some variant of, "I just know it. I feel a free being, I know I'm free. I am free. I know I'm me, and there is only one me. This is who and what I am. Myself. There are no arguments. It's just what is." And without realizing that a millennium and a half ago in India Shankara had written "Everyone knows that he or she exists. No proof is needed. The 'I am' is self-evident." Was Descartes saying the same thing when he wrote "I think, therefore I am" and offered no further proof? Not quite. He was aware of the activities of his mind, whereas Shankara had detected an awareness that seems to lie behind all mental activity and that we believe answers to I.

The Sense of I

This I awareness, as telling what a person understands himself or herself to be, offers itself, especially for us in our time, as the most promising opening into the recesses of the human. Baffling or not, it lies closest to us and brings the fewest presumptions.

In our time almost everyone believes that I is what defines each of us as human. True or not, I obviously has intimately do to with the individual. This is just what must be explored, before more recondite questions arise. Is I all we know about ourselves? How exactly does I behave? How does I maintain its position in the center of our inner life? Is I a fact, or a word, or a mask, or an illusion? Is each I unique as each is certain it is?

Few of us are Shankaras or Descartes, so we are unlikely to discover ourselves as self-evident self-aware, thinking beings. Even I is seldom explicit. I is more inclined to be of a retiring nature most of the time. Like a deer in the forest. Does it become consistently explicit much before we have lived for 8 or 10 years, or more? Of course the word I comes out of a child's mouth early on, but a clear sense of the I as different from all our other ideas and feelings, and the very name of myself in distinction to all other human beings, must be much later. Early teens? If that is so, then coherent individual human experience is possible without an explicit sense of I. This runs counter to our everyday belief that each of us is awarely an I in every situation and would be haplessly adrift if it were not so. But when did everyday beliefs become infallible?

A simple observation to start with: when I is present it need not always be the center of awareness. I can be present though the focus of awareness is the thunderstorm outside. Still, it seems to be the point of reference within our awareness behind which there are no further points of reference. Is it something like the self-identifying locus that each of us carries inside ourselves—the sense of "here is where it's at"? Something like that. But "here is where it's at" is seldom explicit, though virtually always the behavioral pivot of who and where we are. I is more often explicit, yet more often quite absent. How much of the time do we need an I? Need there be an I when one is walking, shaving, eating, reading, enjoying, perceiving, writing, being bored, being sad? There needn't be. I can come and go whimsically, and it does, but is usually not present in our daily habits. Allowing for large differences between individuals.

The words that trickle and bubble out of our mouths as we go about routine activities aren't a reliable indication of the prominence of I. The word "I" is so generally useful it enters of its own accord into countless sentences when, in the awareness of the speaker, there is no explicit sense of I whatsoever. Is this the way it is in boredom, or contentment, or depression? True, in some sense a mood must be some one's. Boredom doesn't waft about, unowned. Though it often seems to lie in the weather or the emptiness of the world as much as in the weather and emptiness of one's feelings. In either case an explicit sense of I is not essential to everyday moods, that's certain.

What about situations in which I does become the dominant player on the stage. We say, "I did it," "I won," "I reached my goal." There's not much doubt about that: I thrusts itself easily and unwilled onto center stage in moments of achievement. The entire experience gathers around one's sense of I, however deceptive such moments may be. Is triumph the high point of I? A long battle against opponents, perhaps enemies, tense uncertainty whether one can bring it off one's own way. And then it happens! The struggle is over! I've done it! Whether in musical or academic competition or in an intense interpersonal struggle in politics or business, triumph must be the crucial experience of I. It may be revenge, merely "I showed him," or it may be a conquest that I believes will be for the common good. But an explicit sense of I-the-doer seems to be integral to the experience. Even in solitude, a flash picturing of a triumph that is still dream, seems to have I at its center.

The other end of the spectrum: whenever there is striving, and failure, I feels hurt. Whether one is belittled professionally or humiliated personally, the resentment or the self-doubt center around an explicit I experience. And in an outright defeat I can be as prominent as it is in triumph. Could the words "humiliation" and "defeat" have meaning without an I humiliated or defeated? It seems that I is required, or believes it is, in decisive moments, good or bad. I is strongly behavioral.

The Sense of Me

Me is something else; of course something more than the grammatical object corresponding to the subject I. Me seems to be almost wilfully illusive and retiring. Not like a deer, but like a nameless mood. At least *my* me eludes me: enjoyable absurdity! Is it that a barely implicit sense of me is closer to the pulsive center of most of our habitual and casual doings than I is? And so closer to one's center of stability? Does me inch into awareness whenever the great mass of body sensations, feelings, and moods that one carries around with one becomes sufficiently prominent to influence behavior? "It seems to me . . , we should not . . . " The me eases itself in and out of our awareness according to need much as I does. Not to the same needs of course. Me is more than a name for oneself. But, like I, it's a will-o-the-wisp.

Me seems to ease itself to the fore when the source of what is happening is experienced as outside myself, as coming toward myself, as affecting myself intimately and often deeply: myself the recipient, not the doer. That seems to be when me takes form to register the feelings, the depth, or personal nature of the experience. "The bear turned on me," not "I was turned on by the bear." "He struck me," not "I was struck by him." "You insult me." These tell clearly of the broad basis of feeling in the me. It need not be specific to be effective. It goes deep and stays in one, often for a long time. If someone says, "I was insulted by him" there is less feeling. It is more retrospective, analytical, more like reporting a fact. Even a more ideational event, "It struck me that we should

. . . ," has more strength in it than, "I had the idea that we should . . . "

I enters, such seems to be its observed wont, when the active, causal pulsion in the situation originates with oneself and is directed toward outward things, "I will tell you tomorrow", or at least away from the I itself, "I am rethinking my attitude toward . . . " Even if it's not a strong assertion or a decision, I claims it for itself: "I prefer eighteenth century music."

Me makes no such explicit claims for itself. Me doesn't think; me doesn't prefer; me doesn't decide. It retires behind I and allows I to claim such activities for itself. Me can be a cunning dissimulator. It provides I with most of the material I "thinks" with. Me names, vaguely, the silent matrix of all sensations and emotions. Fear comes and goes as something in itself, joy and envy the same, but me patiently and with a bottomless depth accepts them all, even if unhappily. Me doesn't choose. Me is the pervading sense that holds individual experience together. Boredom, contentment, such moods are carried by me, not I—usually. Me is the substance of what an individual senses is himself or herself. Yet there are marked differences between one individual and another in the degree of prominence of I and me.

Some of us live in a me-centered world. And others find that their I organizes most of their lives. If me is dominant we may notice a retiring, even a repressed individual. If I spreads its wings over most experience, we may expect self-assertion and a greater degree of self-deception. A strong, explicit me is—without statistical evidence—what holds the individual human together with a sense of his or her own individuality. A sudden awakening to one's own unique, self-subsisting identity is not uncommon: "I suddenly realized, *'I* am *me'*." It would be most odd, impossible perhaps, to say, "My *me* is *I."* That's a delightful riddle. How naturally we can say, "I don't like me." How impossible to say "Me doesn't like I."

What binds a human most closely into his or her world of other people, of things, of other realms of life? I is cool. I holds itself, in degree, aloof from the world around. Me behaves differently. The mood left from the night's dreams merge with me, not I. The mood of the time of day, of one's friends, of one's neighborhood or countryside is not sustained by an aloof I.

The isolated individual has a magical power: it can accept

otherness into itself as its own. How could there be society if this weren't so? We're born with others in our feeling awareness. The gift of sympathy. And moods. That's the me at work. In the evening mood of completion and peace, aren't sky and clouds and trees at peace? What else but the receptive, yearning me could be in tune with the evening? Let I claim the mood for itself: "I am at peace." No matter. It is the me that bears it.

I and Me: Phantoms

Me and I work closely together, but don't claim each other's nature. "*I* have an idea." Who, except a small child, could say, "*Me* has an idea?" It's odd, perhaps—and perhaps not—that me doesn't have ideas. "An idea struck me." Me doesn't claim to have given birth to the idea. I claims the merit of originator. Can I say that me doesn't think? We talk that way, but it's not only ideas that me digests without laying claim to. Emotions are much the same. "Anger overcame me"; but "*I* was angry." I claims the anger, though emotions patently do not arise from the cool I. The nurturing me is content to be the seat of emotions while yielding their title to the loquacious I. That's the way it looks. As if I and me were in collusion to dissimulate. When I says "I", it is often speaking for the retiring me. As Nietzsche put it, Dionysius speaks the language of Apollo. Me holds the greater power, but allows I to be the spokesperson.

Do I say I and me are antipodes? Not quite. Each holds something of the other, or how could they together be the substance of a human individual? If they are that? They're not separable. They're more like two faces of one person. And they're strikingly similar. Each presents itself as unique: there is only *one* I and only *one* me—even for "multiple personalities". They bring this character with them. Neither I nor me could be what it is if there were several of each. I says "I and I alone"; and me says "me and only me." And yet—it must be so—the I in every human being presents itself in precisely the same way: as unique, as unlike any other I there is or ever was. It must be the same for the me. So, riddle on riddle. Every I is the same as every other I, in that each one is unique! And so me.

How grasp this vivially? I and me are singular among all human experiences. Only their close relatives self and own would be comparable. It's a simple given that they are unmistakable. Yet neither has one identifying characteristic! All people recognizes them when they appear, but we can't say how. We can be sure only that we can't describe them. In their everyday presumption they claim to own between them all the experiences a human individual can have—barring a voice from beyond. But their kind of ownership, though totally exclusive, establishes no other bond than that of the experience of the moment. "I was happy." "I was sad." "I was surprised." So I says, but it is not true. Happiness, sadness, surprise were not and did not become qualities of I. Not as we understand a substance and its qualities. How could the one I be both sad and happy? Me will be the same marvel. The sadness, happiness, surprise are experienced as in me, part of me, indeed as me for a brief time. Yet the nature of me is not affected by the me-ness of these experiences. This must be singular. Certainly it baffles. I and me have no other relationship to their experiences than momentary ownership, or perhaps oneness. At least that's the way I take them.

Is I all bombast, pure impostor? Is me merely the owner of what is mine? A further thought. I has at best one power that genuinely belongs to I alone. I can say, "I am aware of my own I." I is claiming to be self-aware. Me does not make the same claim. "Me is aware of me" not only fractures grammar, it cannot be thought. Me is always substance, some weave of feelings and pulsions and doesn't claim to be self-aware. "Me myself" is never spoken except in vernacular word play. "I myself" is common and seems to say that myself is I. It claims a reflexive awareness of I. It is the old historic basis of human uniqueness, and still suspect. The human individual claims to be the only seat of self-awareness, and this claim is then appropriated by I. This does not convince.

But enough of this I-ing and me-ing for now. Soon my I will think it's me, and that would be a disaster. The jungle of these explosive, tiny words hasn't opened up a way into person, but it has shown that the unstable I and the inarticulate me together would make a bizarre and unviable person. Still they're a brother and sister team, marked by the same family character of having no palpable substance. They are more riddle than answer. They claim every idea, passion, mood that comes to an individual's consciousness as their own and yet have no stable natures that allow them to be owners of anything. If no natures, then "I" and "me" name nothing! Yet our life hinges on them.

So far every sentence I've formed about I and me is simply absurd. And that is no fault of language. It's the issue of our faulty expectation. We impose a language developed to deal with existing entities, on what are not existing entities. Every sentence about I or me, however much sense it carries, is strictly unintelligible, simple nonsense. "I am fat." Is I a body?! "I am a farmer." Is I a social, occupational, economic individual of flesh and blood? Such pronouncements begin with I as the immaterial subject, and then smuggle the same I into the sentence a second time, disguised as a flesh and blood object.

This is not simply the problem of all predication: how a substance can be independent of its attributes and yet composed of them. The conundrums of I are of another sort entirely. It's not that I illogically appropriates its attributes as orange or lemon does. It is that it doesn't. And can't. It is that there is no I as the subject-substance of sentences. I is a language impostor. And he fools us all. As does his sister.

Does that mean that I and me are mere metaphors? Some might extricate themselves with that twist. But metaphor as an attribute transferred for a time from its proper place to another subject is, with I and me, transparently useless. I and me do not *exist.* This much is now surely sure. How should we be able to attribute qualities and dispositions to what doesn't exist? Metaphors have little vivial punch.

So. Is this all I can learn from I and me? Can I get nothing at all out of their posturing magic? Well, it's clear they leave many questions about person untouched. It's clear that person can't be merely an I-me being. Yet we breathe them in and out almost every second of our waking lives! They can't be nothing. It's just that they're not what we commonly take them for. I and me bring an unmistakable sense of some presence with them. Else how could we talk back and forth about them? The sense we have of I and me is more immediate, more self-given than any other of our everyday experiences. It is an unique awareness. It stops language dead in its tracks. They are phantoms, will-o-the-wisps, riddles. They've defeated every attempt to treat them as structures or phenomena of consciousness.

Dead end? Not quite. At least I and me have told this I and me much about what a person is not and cannot be. That's a beginning. But how go on?

Don't go anywhere, yet. Stand fast. Listen to the clamor of objections. Indignation. Most will find it absurd, belittling, to reduce the sacred I of the individual Christian and the free-standing citizen of democracy to a phantom. And a posturing, braggart phantom at that. It's self-evident that I is the spiritual center of the individual, caretaker of its soul, the enabling agent of moral responsibility, the sine qua non of person. How could a promise be given, or regret felt if there were no I to redeem the promise or accept the responsibility for regretted mistakes? I makes the legal person possible as well. Away with your I as phantom.

Well spoken. Well meant. This integrates convincingly with our religious and philosophical tradition. Plato's picture of the human as a chariot pulled by two horses, one noble, the other ignoble, and controlled by a charioteer; Augustine's drama of damnation and salvation played out around the self-aware I; the modern conception of the individual as a rational, self-responsible being.

I Not The Seat of Freedom

So be it. But this approved view itself stands in need of fresh questioning. No tradition is the arbiter of vivial truth. There are so many. After all the Buddhist thinks that I, as the word for a self-existent being, is the very pit of ignorance and the greatest obstacle to enlightenment. He never finds it in his own consciousness as an existent something. The Taoists wouldn't find the way that is beyond self-interest the only Way, if they didn't find the individual human naturally aberrant. The Vedantic understanding of the I shares the merits of Buddhism and the Christian West, but becomes dogmatic. That they see "I-the-doer" as an illusion is attractive. Of course, they go further and insist that the world must be false if I's actions in it are illusory. That's intriguing too. But when they transparence the I into the presence of absolute truth—*Brahman*—they become dogmatic. The I does act as a kind of mask for other powers, true. But it's not clear yet what such other powers might be. If it ever can be.

These remote remembrances will not satisfy the doubters, nor should they. There is something self-evident about the I. We feel the excitement, the power, of I making life decisions out of its own freedom. We feel we are free beings. Where there is conflict, doubt, guilt, where something must be done, I may appear to be in the center of the decision, asserting its freedom and accepting the responsibility. Where else could freedom have its seat but in the I that is unique in every human? In most cases though I is not the explicit, self-aware I of the textbook. In times of conflict the internal shoving and tugging goes on without the need for a strong I to appear. It could get in the way. I can become more than Sartre's "opaque area". It can become a dark patch blotting out the incipient insights and judgments that a crisis stirs into life. It can obstruct the new ideas and horizons that have been set free in one. All emerging situations have moral implications, but the I is not needed to make the decisions. We seem to live our way through crises thanks to valuations that arise unwilled. Sometimes we say "conscience". What a putdown of all the other powers of an individual if the I alone were to make decisions of moral significance!

Wouldn't it make more sense to recognize our ever-present value sense and conscience as the governing influence and substance of an individual? They structure our problems in their light and shade and so induce appropriate decisions and actions. This appropriateness appears in our awareness as "the decision", which I so often claims for itself. The happening is more like an acceptance of the valuations one's nature brings to bear. And not even this acceptance is an "act of decision". It's simply accepting responsibility for one's own way of being.

But the doubter insists that human freedom means freedom of the will as realized in the decisions of I. This thought has a long history. But I can do no other than to see it as a confusion of freedom with responsibility. It has been fired to new strengths by our modern deification of the I-centered person. Would I dare say bluntly that the human individual is not free? Well, if someone holds that freedom is the property of a self-existing being that shapes its destiny through decisions awarely taken in full responsibility by its I, then I say, no the human individual is not free.

Must human actions then be determined? Are human "decisions" formed before they are taken? No, of course they're not. The doubters will corner me: what third possibility is there between freedom and nonfreedom? None, if freedom is to be an attribute of self-conscious decisions and nothing more. But is freedom no more than that? Must freedom be grasped as a specific attribute of a very specialized kind of conscious act squeezed into emerging life situations? Does freedom have its only seat in "acts of decision"?

What a puny freedom that would be. It's closer to life to see freedom as the own-most nature of a being. Not an attribute of some part or a special function, but inseparable from the being's being. Of a being who has the potency to hear the silent voices that come from its own source of vivial worth, however inarticulate they may be. This would mean that a human individual is "free" as a being who has the potency of a spontaneity always greater than the "realities" of any situation he or she find themselves in. Only this, however one says it, makes it thinkable that humans could be free from the stultification of body, of mind, of habit, of beliefs, and of historical and economic limitations. Freedom can enter any situation as this spontaneity.

So, the discomfiting outcome: I is not the heart-core of our moral decisions. I is itself neither moral nor immoral. I is able to persuade us, as a monarch stripped of his powers continues to parade and posture for his subjects, that it possesses our moral sense and makes decisions on our behalf. But that just doesn't seem to be the way it is. I is as little able to establish itself as the key in matters of moral choice, as it was in matters of ideas and feelings and moods. That is sure. I is prominent in giving voice to the constancy of person. Yet it turns out to be a phantom in consciousness, a great promise that evanesces on being put to the test. This is a harsh putdown of the universally revered I. But I is so much less the key to person than we believe. And it is a tortuous way to search for person. There must be more promising ways.

But not throwing the I out. The idea of constancy derives its sense from a nonontic center in the individual. The sharpest voice of this sense is the irrepressible I. Regrets and promises can be what they are only as the regret experienced or the promise given by someone. And that someone recognizes himself or herself most commonly in the thought: "I did it"; "I regret it"; "I promised"; "I will keep the promise". I isn't the stable individual. But stability can't be understood if a regret or a promise are not "of" an individual who recognizes himself or herself as such. The sense of I may focus such recognition. But a sense of being one's own self is present in the background as a guarantee. This must be so. I is certainly not the creative center of an individual. And yet . . . I won't go away. It must be an essential piece in the puzzle. At least it's a degree of clarification to discover I without its royal robes and crown of selfhood. I is thin gruel if offered as oneself.

Self

Self: that word has been ghosting about in the background during all this talk about I. And hasn't been invited to speak up. "Self" is one of the most ancient of words clustered around the human individual. And it never speaks of anything less than one's ownness, the own-most part of oneself. Self somehow holds I and me together. Not just "myself" but one's own very self. That the Greeks didn't recognize this sense of the word is a striking comment on their outward turned realism. Even Socrates spoke only of myself or yourself, not of "the" self.

That the word "self" is circulating among us today is evidence of a flickering sense that the human individual is more than genes and psychic states. And, as far as may be, it is being used to counter the dominant behaviorist, physiological, and social construct understanding of humans that encloses us. Self is lonesome and falls into strange hands: from magazine publishers who coach young folk in the wiles of Freudian libido to psychic mediums who put believers into touch with their "higher selves". But it needn't remain there. At least it's a recognition that a human being is not to be explained by the physical laws that form crystals and human bodies; and that deserves encouragement. Though it is often one-sidedly subjective, self points toward a center of forces other than physical or vital. Today we are so deeply into the myth of cultural individualism, freedom, and psychoanalytical ego theory that self often becomes the strongest available word for the individual ego.

Of course it's not put that way. "Self" is a loftier word than "I", but often there is not other distinction between them.

Vivial problems have strange biographies. Classical Taoists seem to have had no explicit vocabulary for this problem, even though their primary concern was to discourage the individual from acting out of purely individual interest. The Greeks don't help directly, except to tell us that they didn't need the problem. The late antique Gnostics do, though their language is not ours. Still, the divine light that they hold to be the hidden spark of liberation in the individual seems a strong metaphor for what we might say with self. And that human existence consists of the struggle to free this spark to merge with the divine light itself reads like a translation into religious language of the more sober conception of the classical Sanskrit thinkers. But Yajnavalkya's Upanishadic simplicity and depth are singular. The way he refuses every name and every attribute for one's self, until finally, in a flash of realization, one sees that the self is not an inner object of consciousness, but the awareness that describes all things, excepting only itself. Self can never become an object of knowledge because it is always the knower, distinct both from the world of objects and from the contents of the individual mind. This is not congenial to everyone and is without our naturalist pale of propriety. But fascinating because no Western thinker has attempted so directly to ground the self in the behavior of philosophical reflection. When Yajnavalkya took a second gigantic step, and pronounced the self of the individual, so discovered, to be none other than Being and Truth, the great universal *Brahman* present in all beings and in all things, classical Indian thought was complete. Self is not an individual being. It is cosmic! Not exactly our common view today.

Were ever two contradictory ideas so inextricably interwoven as Yajnavalkya's and Buddha's? Yajnavalkya's use of the common conviction that one's I is one's self guided his investigation into the "true" self: the latter being recognized as the former is dissipated. The individual I, though an illusion, was still a feeble pretense of the "true" self and so helpful as a learning device. Buddha's repudiation of the very notions of I and self had to yield another result. They were common ignorance. Did he have a deep fear of them? They were to be uprooted and thrown away. So, as the enlightened individual had been deprived of an I and denied a universal self, what else could follow but that what presenced after the I and self of ignorance had vanished—*nirvāṇa*—had no relation to individual existence in the space-time cosmos? *Nirvāṇa* was neither true, nor true being, nor did it explain anything. It was simply the end of the illusion of individual existence, an ascetic outcome of ascetic striving.

But a seed bed of other conceptions. Later Buddhism is more interesting. Enlightenment seems more plausible than *nirvāṇa*. As the I and the self, still feared as the deep pits of ignorance, weaken, the individual discovers the Buddha nature—perfect peace—in himself or herself. And then such individuals move through the world bringing this freedom and wisdom with them. He or she is not destined to vanish from human society. Behavior takes the place of meditation as the crucial concept. Enlightenment is not the end, but becomes the way of being of an enlightened human.

This is powerful thinking. But the striking point: that the behavioral stability of such a one lies not in an I or self, but in enlightenment, which is precisely the going beyond both these.

Nietzsche's Life-Body

Such notions are remote from the Western tradition and from our public beliefs today. But Nietzsche is able to argue that the self—his *Selbst—is* at the heart of a living individual. His rejection of Kant's scientific and Christian exploration of the self gathered so much momentum he found himself pronouncing for its opposite: self as *Leib,* self as the voice of life that reached him through his body. His claim to find his self in his impulses, his appetites, his unnameable urge to create has to be the most startling statement about person in Western thought. Kant's theoretical reason, so complacently self-sufficient in its own made-for-science laws, just had to provoke Nietzsche into passionate protest. The way he makes Kant's pure reason into his own "little reason", impotent in life questions, exactly where his own "great reason", the voice of his self, was sovereign, has a touch of word play and parody in it. Nietzsche's wit was his strongest weapon. He must have felt Kant was betraying the living earth, the only home worthy of his life-body. It's tempting to see Freud's *Id* in Nietzsche's great reason, but a comparison would spoil both. Nietzsche's great reason is not unconscious. It is the feel of life forces, as they seep into consciousness with their dumb messages, that form the great reason. The individual configuration of these forces is, in each case, the self. Startling. Nietzsche must have been the first Ph.D. in Europe to put his life forces above his intellect. But he would have been untrue to his German language if he had not found a high place for *Geist:* spirit-intellect. He seems to have been sure that personal transformation took place in the realm of *Geist.* It had to be rooted in life-body change of course, but given lasting form in spirit.

What can I learn from Nietzsche? Well, he's a life-saving counter to European rationalism. Its understanding of the way ideas live within the intellect as citizens in a privileged realm results in starving humans of life food, just what Nietzsche was searching for. He turned away from intellectual and moral conventions and even from conventional language. A promising direction, for sure. But still only a direction, with much left unclarified. Self as body rubs out so much that is essential to the individual. Is there only one source of sense open to us? What of life values that would curb and reform "body" wisdom? Without them we have only the rump of a human. Life-body is a restricting sense of the way of all things.

Body

But Nietzsche is the breach in the European wall of the intellect. He brought body back into the concept of the human. Odd how difficult it is to move outside the rigid presumptions of one's own time. European rationalists and Christians saw body and mind as antipodes: the one spiritless flesh and the other fleshless spirit. But their medicinal cousins thought differently. Their theory of the four "humors" is so sure that a human is of one nature. For medicine, four liquids: blood, phlegm, yellow bile, and black bile. For ordinary folk including poets and playwrights, four temperaments: sanguine, phlegmatic, choleric, and melancholic. The words were parallel, telling the belief that a human was not a dualism of body and mind, but was one being with four principles.

But that is no longer our public belief. Intellect has become independent and imperialistic; body has become independent and biochemical, threatening to take over the realm claimed by the intellect. Our presumptions now compel us to look for causal explanations of the ways body influences mind and mind, body. This must be a unique presumption. We would brush off as nonsense the Taoist refusal to separate the *Te,* the great Way's power in the individual, into physical and mental attributes: his conviction that the individual was one and whole. And how much more nonsensical is the Buddhist view that the body is the seat of thirst for all perishable things and after enlightenment becomes the locus of the Buddha's imperishable being! And the derision of our biochemists if they were ever to hear of the Upanishadic view that the body is an illusory construct in an illusory physical world, the "own" body of an illusory individual mind! Even the latest attempts to integrate body and mind through the device of systemic wholeness does little justice to the classical views. How could it? The notion of a system of dynamic forces internally coherent is derived from our physical sciences. To attempt to extend that notion into the area of persons and self-aware vivial experiences doesn't rescue the mind, it includes the mind in the body world. End of person.

Whatever the great ones say, our bodies are still with us, in some way or perhaps many ways ineluctably part of the weave of the everyday. Theories come easily once we have accepted the language of "body" and "mind". But is this justified vivially? How does body appear in the everyday, and what functions does it have? What are we talking about when we say "body", especially "my body"? A hackneyed convention? Spontaneous experiences?

So the first question has to be, How do we discover our bodies? Do we ever become aware of our bodies as whole, as separate from ourselves and yet our own? That is, do I ever experience my body as not *me?* As not *mine?* As an indifferent object? The answer must be no, disregarding out-of-body experiences. Most commonly we are aware of parts of our bodies: the face we see in the mirror, shaving or washing; what makes trouble from time to time: headache, sore back, broken leg; eliminatory and sexual parts. And even so they are seldom mere objects of flesh. It's the sensations and feelings coming to us from them that absorb our attention: the ache in the head, the pain in the back, the hunger and thirst in the trunk, tiredness and the relaxed ease after a massage, the nausea after bad food or drink. And then the fascinating way we have of assimilating virtually all such body feelings to our I or me, leaving the body part merely their locus or a naming of their specific nature. My head doesn't have an ache, I have the headache; my back doesn't have a sore, I have a sore back; my body isn't hungry or thirsty, I am; my body isn't tired, I am; my body isn't relaxed after a massage, I am; my stomach isn't nauseated, I am. My body doesn't even see or hear; I do that. And not my body, but I, am old or young, ugly or handsome.

So. The possessive I is taking charge again. Good thing. How else live the unity of body and mind? Rather, how else can a human being be one being, and not two? Of course I is just a front man, but what else could do it? The sense of ownness that is sometimes in the background is not explicit or embracing. The I and the me are not separated from their body. And most conscious life is, in some degree, an expression of a diffuse body presence. We live as one being. Decisions seem to be taken with all of me, not just my mind. And most enjoyments resonate through my whole being. The body is alive and lives the feelings seeping into even the least of its members. *I* have a pain in my little toe. So we live in pleasure or pain as one being.

Illusion? It must be. How can a nonexistent I and a fraudulent mind have a body? How can I say "my body"? Are bodies not blobs of biochemistry? And is mind not conscious experience that has no existence in the world of natural processes? Mind and body contradict each other, if we define them so that they must. Yet they live together naturally and make an individual human being possible. We are astonished that will-o-the-wisps I and me can assimilate body sensations and feelings as their own, indeed that they come to sense who and what they are in virtue of them. But they do, and that is vivially decisive. So, ungraspable, but not an illusion. There can't be an I and a me without a body for them—not in the only world we know. Can I imagine myself in another body? Would I still be me if I found myself in a 30-year-old, 300-pound body? That's unbelievable. Even more so if it were a female body.

Well then, quite simply, mind and body are inseparable. A mind needs a body. And more: only I can live with my body. The quality of my conscious experiences are, I do believe, unique to my metabolism, blood, muscle tone or lack of it, bone structure, muscle texture—running was so easy, lifting wasn't—the specific virtues of my body senses—sharp vision, dull taste—even my illnesses and surgical experiences. All this nurtures my I and me to much of their essential nature.

But one's value sense? Could one show that Plato's idealism was integral to Plato's body and Aristotle's realism to his? No. That would make no sense. Valuing is a different kind of experience than body sensing. And vivial experience doubly so. The specific forms they take are certainly not dependent on the specific body character of the person involved. Obese energetic men may be raw sensualists or great idealists. Or both. And yet, valuing and vivial sensing—the full range of person experience—are possible only for a being with an integrated I-me body. The oceans of mind-body arguments depend on how one sets up their dichotomy. Gene theory can't help. Value experience can't be analyzed in the same terms as body cells.

Nietzsche started this. But I don't find, as he did, that I am "wholly and solely my body". It's just that we can be the kind of being we are, only because the body gives "I" and "me" a life locus where they can be what they are. That puts an end to the belief that one's *individual* soul lives on after the death of its body. And to the Vedantic dogma that the individual is pure spirit linked with a body only by the illusion of I and mine. It leaves us with what we are able to discover about and make out of ourselves. We needn't curse our fate because we are burdened with bodies. That is what we are, and what we have to make the best of. No escape. What to do but accept the unrequested task of a life that must search for itself through the absurdity of a rootless I and me and a given body nature? We are ignorant folk, soaked in imperfection, who can do no more than try to keep our imperfections from suffocating us.

But this brings me no closer to breaking open the mystery of I and me. Where do they come from? What is it that must search for itself behind I and me?

Kant and Self

Kant's answer is the clearest and most self-assured in Western thinking. And the most sharply opposed to what makes sense to me. The great man's thinking is too intricate to be countered easily.

But he bites deeply into two or three puzzles that have much to say about vivial exploration and the idea of a person.

Kant's attempt to grasp the self as the enabling presumption of the unity of all knowledge does not convince me. What human being could unify all knowledge? Which of us can even move from one body of knowledge to another without bringing one's rooted perspective, one's unaware values with one? What remains of a self that enables the possibility of something that never happens? Kant's hope that when one is aware of the I as the logical center of all knowledge, one will realize that one *is* this very power oneself. It's a breathtaking idea. Makes one dizzy. The self of an individual, one's very own self, is the reference point for all possible scientific propositions! This transcendental I can of course never be found by merely studying the contents of the mind. It makes knowing possible, but can itself never be known.

This is Kant's self, in theoretical aspect. But it is not the self we must live with. It offers us no sure center for living. It doesn't reconcile body and mind. It doesn't account for the intuitive way we have of understanding one another. How does it concern us? It's more a theory of the natural sciences than of the human person. It leaves the flesh and blood and emotions and thought of human life out of account. Universal science is not what we *live* by. Once again self as the nature of person has proved to be something of a dead end. It falls an easy victim to the demands of dogmatism. It closes in on itself prematurely.

That the human has an affinity for powers and regions beyond one's individual nature is a great and classic thought of Kant's. But to confine them within an eighteenth century theory of science doesn't help us very much any more. Nor did it satisfy Kant. He still had reason in its practical use up his sleeve. And that's more promising.

The way Kant's presumption of a supranatural rational self fuses with his full-blooded experience of a sense of duty in the famous dictum, "The moral law is a given fact," is the key. And fascinating. Because Kant's moral will was rationality in practice, it could will only what every other rational will would will in the same circumstances. So a rational will—how powerful that word "rational" was in Kant's time—could will only the highest good. Wonderful how few proofs we need in these questions. Understanding how we live is the key. Kant's seminal experience seems to be the spontaneity of the human will, its power to originate action not only independent of the inclinations of the senses, but directly counter to them. This astounding freedom arises in the midst of physical objects obedient to the laws of nature. It gives Kant the key to human nature in action.

When Kant sets up his three "postulates" of the moral will—freedom, immortality, and the existence of god—in effect the structure of the moral universe, it is telling that he says we can never know them to be true, but only that the moral law empowers us to "take them as true". The postulates are the conditions necessary for the highest good to be possible. So Kant puts it. The moral will could not exist in a universe empty of the postulates. But they are justified and sustained by the experience of the universality of the moral ought as a fact.

Kant is a turning point in modern European thought. His treatment of reason in its vivial uses is just as rationalist as his treatment of scientific reason, it is true. But glowing through his elaborate vocabulary is the pure experience of a very sensitive and plain-thinking man. The moral will rises spontaneously to answer the imperative of human freedom in the face of all circumstance. To make this the source of his search for the best sense of things in a human world is his finest merit. Throughout he is exploring the horizons of the human person.

It is the earthy experience of the imperative of duty, the moral ought, that brings a sense of freedom. And the notion of a spontaneous and free will obviously sanctions the determination to fulfill the duty. Following the call of duty is freely willing the moral nature of a person. And reciprocally, the idea of freedom is secured in that behavior. The other postulates make vivial sense as well—if we accept Kant's Christianity. The postulates of the existence of a god who sustains the moral law and of eternal life in which the human may fulfill that law derive from the moral behavior of the person, even as they illuminate it. Whether we accept Kant's starting point or not needn't affect what we can learn from him.

Kant's conception of the person as a being of pure rational spirit unencumbered by external sense organs, extreme as it is, still teaches much. It grounds his seminal notion that the human person should never be treated as a means to an end, but always as an end in itself. That alone makes it a precious passage in Western thought.

And yet, Kant makes it clear. Self brings its own problems as a way to grasp person. There's something self-defeating about the very notion. It's too exclusive. It's complacent, final. It implies a being that is a whole, not caused by anything outside it. It must be its own law-giver. This is a mighty thought. But how could such a being have anything to do with a mere human individual, that notoriously imperfect creature? How picture such a self integrating flexibly with one's confused motives, with one's contradictory aesthetic enjoyments, with one's amorphous and shifting sense of the way of things? How could such a self ever be the living heart of a human individual? Self is too perfect for this world. It is a dogmatism let loose too early. "Self" is an end-of-the-road term. It stops further investigation. A touch-stone perhaps, a provocation to a more critical study of the individual, a sharp push in a certain direction of thought. But not a being to be discovered and lived with.

The Sense of Own

So, farewell to self. But there's something unsaid. There is more to self than a smug, self-existent being. "Self" is a substance word we never encounter squarely; it eludes us. And yet there is a sense that does reach deep down and far back, that is pervasive and more often present than I or me. It is not obtrusive, not a substance. It is more an adjective, a quality. It does more for the stability of the individual than any other factor in the complex life of consciousness and body. It is the nonontic orienting center of a person's world. It is the nonspatial midpoint of the spatial world. It is the simplest, most embracing notion we have. And the most baffling: the sense of *own.*

Not own in the sense of possession; more own as uncaused, underived, as recognizing whatever is felt to be own, but not mine. It is the presence of a spontaneous, mysterious worth that suffuses one's inner indefinably. It embraces I and me without speaking their language. It lies deeper. It is the end discovery in the individual human. It is not a neutral or distant awareness of ourselves. It is the closest sense of ourselves we can have. It discovers and sanctifies the individual, telling its unique worth.

But the contradiction! Ownness is awareness that by self-definition is awareness of an individual by an individual. It's not an individual's creation or possession. Awareness is common to all humans and unnumbered other species. Yet this awareness is sensed as own, as singular. It's the discovery of the individual's existence. Where does ownness come from? How think the ownness of own as singular me and as equally singular for every human? Impossible. Impossible to *think* own, but impossible to doubt it. How does it come to be at home in every individual human consciousness? Or should the question be, Is the individual's home not in oneself, as individual, at all? Could we be supraindividual creatures? What status to allow own? Magic?

Now I see how the Upanishadic thinkers could be so obsessed with the problem of the individual's natural belief that the consciousness available to one is one's own. They came face to face with this deepest, most obvious conviction any human can have and, being the thinkers they were, had to account for it. Which they did—to their satisfaction. Their belief in a cosmic spirit present in every individual made an answer possible. The individual makes a profound mistake: one believes the cosmic spirit present to one is one's own I-me consciousness. And so the illusory ego is born, and the illusory world is on its way. The problem is solved. Pure genius. But, how account for the illusion itself? Is it just a mistake? Unthinkable. Every creature suffers from the identical illusion. The Indians saw the problem clearly. It's the dogmatism of the cosmic spirit that is too much. We can be sure only of our encounter with pure awareness, and the sense of own that nestles silently in its midst and abides there, without passport or title to its place. That is the magic. But it's no illusion. And it is no solution. It survives outside of solutions—for us.

Aware Behavior

So be it. However, there's more to self and own than magic, though magic they are. We live in the pulsive turmoil of behavior. If person is to allow us a glimpse of itself, it will have to be from that battle scene, or I won't be able to believe it. Does some fellow feeling with Kant's behavioral puritanism make me assume that behavior is the scene where we can best test all questions? And with Nietzsche's belief that ideas are to be lived for their worth? Both are very close to my "aware behavior"—the notion that has survived destruction so far and must be explored on the way to person.

What would I be trying to say with "aware behavior"? Well this much: the philosophers' theories about the way of things cannot be true. They are withdrawn from the lived matrix where they were born and where they made sense: the inner behavior of the philosopher with his ideas, because thinking is one kind of inner behavior. It involves value judgments, a sense of direction, decision. But it isn't aware behavior. Mostly thinking is akin to painting or composing music. The thinker has to be aware of the ideas developing in the mind as having their own life, if he or she is to be critical of them. One's awareness is distinct from what one is aware of. In aware behavior it isn't. The experience ceases to be the object of inner observation. The awareness is inherent in the experience; it merges with it. Object and subject are foreign to it. Knowing loses its customary sense.

Well, that's some thing like it. What can be set aside as not being aware behavior? It's not an intuition as insight into something. And it's not merely knowing what one is doing. "I'm playing chess", "I'm reading Plato" are not examples of aware behavior. More incisive is the absence of the I-me, especially of I-the-doer. But there is such a range of experience without an explicit I. Is aware behavior the same as non-I behavior?

That would be meaningless. Aware behavior wants to lie very close to the singular way in which person is present. So the absence of an explicit I in our daily habits—dressing, eating, driving the car—does not make them into aware behavior. What about the times one is sunk in concentration on critical passages in a chess match or watching some sports or theatrical spectacle? We say we are absorbed or enraptured. But typically absorption or rapture are experiences in which what one is doing, or watching, holds the full stage; one's awareness of what one is experiencing is feeble or disappears entirely. But aware behavior suggests the equal presence of both. The possibilities narrow.

Composing music, writing poetry, or exploring ideas are

among the most enlightening experiences a human can have. Yet they are not quite aware behavior. They must have a medium in which to work that is outside the individual: language, tones, ideas. Their effort is, in some degree, willed. The individual is not far removed from the work. He or she is always reshaping his or her own experience, but always through a medium. Aware behavior, as I say it, works with no medium other than a person's experience. It's a kind of unwilled discovery. There can be no distance between person and the experience. Art can be rapturous, but still not aware behavior.

What about vivial exploration itself: the experience of transparencing everyday reality into the life sense it so effectively covers over? What is going on when physical, measurable space transparencies into the openness of the life-giving boundless? This is not quite the experience of Archimedes or Newton, but is it in its own modest way a kind of aware behavior? Well, how? Physical space contradicts the vivial worth of boundlessness, yet leads one to it, even while sustained as a useful belief, though not a reality that can be known as an object. The nonexistent physical space, in being transparenced, allows its opposite—nonphysical spacelessness—to presence. The boundless arises out of the measurable! The paradox is the key. And is lived in its patent incomprehensibility only as paradox.

Is that aware behavior? Can the sense of it be separated from the behavior of the discovery? And is the behavior of the discovery separable from its sense? No, neither is. But, even now I'm *thinking* about the sense of boundlessness without the initial behavior of discovery. That's so. But thinking will not recover that experience. This will hold for any experience that doesn't concern mere facts. Words will attempt to evoke the experience subsequently, but cannot ever validate or invalidate it. Buddha discovered *nirvāṇa,* Plato the idea of the good. Each gave an account of his experience afterward. Buddha said the imperishable had been attained; Plato said the idea of the good was the source of both knowledge and its truth. Only those who believe that in their own way they have made the same discovery can judge its worth. The rest of us are merely disputing theories. The experience subsequently embodied in words remains immune to detached theory. It retains its worth, in the face of all theory. It may alter its significance only after other or greater aware behavior. In this sense aware behavior is irrefutable. It's the detached reasonings offered that are.

And so, in their own way, with the explorations of time, words, knowing, inner, and outer. They qualify, but on the fringe. Mostly though, aware behavior becomes real in life crises: when the shaping notion of ourselves we've been living with is falling apart, and fresh impulses are struggling to tell us what to do. How often in the late thirties or early forties life tries to disintegrate what there is of us. There's a temptation to desert one's family or to renounce one's faith or homeland; or there is a sudden threat of early death or perhaps the horrible realization that nothing is going to happen. One's habitual motives and values can turn upside down and show us the revolting underside we had successfully kept hidden from ourselves. Perhaps it is that the hypocrisy of high purpose has been suffocating a modest talent or that lack of courage has hidden a greater talent. There will be a turmoil of discovered false motives, tentative fresh hopes that may be equally false, lack of trust in one's own honesty. Yet the presence of a new life whispers wordlessly on the fringes of awareness. And takes form as a firm but undefined sense of where one ought to be heading. And one accepts that, lets it become clear enough to allow one to say, I'll go; or, I can't do that; or, let me just not be a coward; or, well, life is fecund, for me too.

What's striking at such times is the absence of clear ideas, feelings, and images that one could recognize and name and base decisions on. There could be no motives, no goals, certainly no reasoning to clarify the confusion and shape its sense. We can never say afterward, I made a decision. Not until after the crisis itself has taken decisive form. The experience is both one's emerging inner behavior and one's awareness of that. The two are one, certainly inseparable. I-the-doer isn't present. If one were to invite I to make the decisions it would disrupt the emerging sense of one's new life. Nameless discoveries that arise by themselves are far wiser than one's I. Nietzsche's "great reason" is close to this.

The significance and worth of what is going on in the crisis is one with the sense of what is going on. One's inner behavior *is* this sense; and this sense is the only form the inner behavior could take. To say it again, what one goes through in any aware behavior can *be* only in one's own understanding of it. Or again, knowing transmutes into inner behavior, and behavior becomes the path of knowing. What happens to truth in this account? What if one's understanding is false? Meaningless question. Whatever emerges later as a reasoned account can never alter the experience itself. Aware behavior is irrefutable. It should claim no truth, for there is nothing for it to be true of.

That's quite a bundle of words about an experience that is itself wordless, essentially. So, this must be clear: my words don't describe aware behavior. That would be impossible. Words are the nudges and reminders and guiding suggestions for finding the experience. But they don't lead the mind through its meanings. They are to be lived. The wise used to say, "The one is known by many names." And "aware behavior" is one of the many names that may be used for the classical experience of a seminal awakening. Buddha's invitation to any and all to test the claims of his teaching by undergoing the same experience he had, marks aware behavior. There was no invitation to debate theories. Hui Neng's statement is equally direct: the behavior of meditation cannot be separated from insight into the Buddha's truth; they are one. And the Christian belief that one who begs forgiveness honestly will feel the healing hand of god in his own heart assumes the self-clarifying nature of that behavior.

The Chinese and Japanese koan is an ancient and tested training method. The teacher's refusal to expound theory separated from the student's own experience makes koan resolution aware behavior. A beginner who asks, "What is the Buddha nature?" and is told, "Three baskets of rice," confronts an absurdity that is as real as his or her own breathing. The teacher's relentless insistence and the beginner's own will together help the beginner find a way of shattering the absurdity of any attempt at explanation. No theory will do: no concept of mystical presence in all things, no concept of transcendence, no concept of immanence removes the absurdity. Only for one who finds out how to live in the Buddha's way can the absurdity of "three baskets of rice" transmute into the aware behavior of an awakening.

Lao Tzu and Chuang Tzu never tire pointing out the kinds of behavior required of one who would understand the Way—aware behavior. Chuang Tzu's dictum "The finest understanding is the understanding that understands nothing" emphasizes the absence of subject and object in the experience. And then there's Carl Jung's exploration of the problem in his psychological way. His "individuation" has a lot in common with what aware behavior is trying to get at. When he says we can uncover the unconscious forces that disguise themselves as our own ego and can learn to shift the center of our awareness to accept these factors as integral to a new "self", Jung implies a new center in the person. That too is a type of aware behavior. Jung's emphasis on the inexplicability of the transformation is the bey. Aware behavior is a radical discovery, a kind of awakening. The new is always a transforming of the old. The new has no readymade place in language and defies explanation. Some kinds of experience are ever new: the way a friend becomes a loved person.

Can there be something in common among the Zen koan, the Taoist "understanding that understands nothing", Jung's individuation, and—of all things—scientific inspiration¿ Well they all have a long struggle with confusing and irreconcilable ideas. The scientist clearly so. And then comes the moment when years of frustration suddenly clarify into an answer, usually a simple one, as if it had dropped in by itself. Archimedes runs out of the bathhouse without bathrobe shouting, "*Eureka,* I've found it": the principle of volume displacement. Isaac Newton sits in his garden and the sea of conflicting data from physics and astronomy suddenly clarifies into one simple idea: gravity. Of course the scientist gains a formula for this idea that can be passed on. The others do too. An account is always given, subsequently. But what is the experience of the scientific discovery¿ Is that an experience in which the behavior of thinking is inseparable from its meaning¿ Is it a passing fade-out of subject and object¿ I hope it is. It throws a broader light on aware behavior.

Is it too broad¿ After all previous ages didn't focus on the same problems we do. There is a common base, true. But the cosmos of ideas and resolutions that classical ages had to make their sense is not our own. Indeed our peculiarity is that we have no cosmos of ideas—only a chaos. So the grand sense-bringing ideas of *nirvāṇa, Brahman, tao,* idea of the good, creator god cannot honestly bring a resolving sense to the wordless experiences of aware behavior in our own time. They are answers that conclude all vivial puzzlement; they are dogmas, immune to alteration.

We have none such. None that can survive vivial exploration. For us ignorance is never rooted out, not cleanly and totally. Ignorance defines our human being. Our enlightenment is more or less and always open to fresh experience. We can't realize more than a handmade vivial stance. To believe we can is ignorance. We must look toward more modest possibilities: crises in our personal lives, moments of wordless learning from nature, the revelation of personhood, the discovery of a sustaining life sense.

Aware behavior has lots of bone and gristle, but a few solid bites for the exploration of person. It's a fragment of a morphology of human experience. So much I'll hold onto. Aware behavior is a sensing that is the same as what is being sensed: no subject, no object. It is neither intuition nor action. It is not the presence of an idea. It is the chunkiest, most concrete experience we can have. It skirts the fringes of language. It gives birth to its own kind of modest awakening. But is not mysticism, having no transcendental object.

Individual and Society

Aware behavior brings out a capacity in the individual that opens the way to person. Without it the sense that the word "person" carries could not show. But, by itself, aware behavior could overemphasize the aloneness of person and that would be an elemental misconception. Person isn't the handsomely sculpted figure of a lone individual polishing his or her vivial stance. It's overwhelmingly plain that other people inhabit one's own awareness. To look for person as an isolated being, understandable within itself, would be not to look for person at all. Still, to explore the individual, the irreducible carrier of human life, seemed the only way to look for person. What else but a human individual, in his or her most special power, could sense the worth of life? It's that power that points to person.

Yet again the hunger for vivial nourishment is formed—not implanted—by the people and language and religion one grows into. Kant's penetration to the vivial is a fascinating marriage of his radical Christianity and eighteenth century physics. Plato's penetration is a marriage of the Greek cosmos, humanly meaningful, the Greek urge to explain all things, and his own experience of the way the human mind falls heir to its ideas. And from the commonplace: boyhood years playing hockey and running races on the street in front of a wooden Methodist church. And at university discovering Plato with an Oxford scholar.

Individual awareness seems by its nature to be awareness of other people. We are born into a world of other people and become aware of ourselves primarily through discovering our like and dislike of others and their disapproval or approval of us. Other people, certainly family, are part of oneself. Their natures seem to seep into the me labyrinth and find a home there. And so it is with things and landscape and the words we hear and use. All are within us. All share in one's sense of life worth. Words most especially live only by being shared. What word can be spoken, even in soliloquy, without its sense being open for sharing? And beneath the words the age-old enthrallments of one's people quietly spread their roots: Christianity, the Greeks as the only "classical" people, history as progress, scientific democracy as its fulfillment.

And yet, the individual is not a "product" of his or her society, not even an "artifact". It's more that the encounter with the otherness of other humans throws one back on oneself. It's more that the discovery of one's ownness, of the inner space where I and me are the prominent voices, is the natural sequel to the first experience of oneself as something apart from the surrounding social weave.

That is bedrock. I can't believe we would ever explore ourselves if other people hadn't awakened us to ourselves; and not just to ourselves as someone with such and such a temperament or character. If inner and outer are inseparable we cannot discover ourselves as persons except through the presence of another person. The discovery of oneself as a person is other than to become aware of oneself as an individual. For merely to exist in society it is enough to have discovered oneself as an individual. To discover oneself as a person is something else.

The Discovery of Person

Person says more than individual. There was no clarity or resting place in the I-me sense of ourselves, nor in the moral stability that binds past and future to the present, nor in any version of the self. All this still left a sense of something missing. It seemed to draw a magic circle around the individual's sense of himself or herself as a self-sufficient unit of society. But that leaves out the need of the individual for a sense of life, of the way it is with all things, the need to live in a meaningful cosmos. That's certain. But strictly inconceivable. Ancient and modern great thinkers have offered their understanding of the relationship between individual and cosmos, but none has made it thinkable. Which doesn't make it any less the crux of human life.

How can this insoluble mystery show itself plainly? None of my probings into the individual found a person that of its own nature could have access to a sense of all things. The inexplicable, but inalienable, sense of ownness grounds the individual. And that frustrates any relationship to the nature of things. Of course the Upanishadic thinkers found the universal spirit of things in a transformed individual, as did the Buddhists. But their discoveries drew the story of the person to a close, if a grand one: no further questions. And Kant's person depends heavily on the presumptions of the Christian religion. How can we, in our time, find in the individual human a potence to transparence the insoluble absurdities of an individual's relation to the way of all things?

Well, that almost intimidates one into silence. But there's a different way of putting the question. What is it that gives us a sense of the presence in the individual of a range of worth beyond the survival interests of an individual? A range of worth that can awaken the belief that a sense of the way of all things has been vouchsafed us somehow? Nothing like this showed up in the introspective search of the individual. But experience justifies the question. As a person one speaks confidently of life sense.

The I-me uniqueness marks us off against the world and against other humans. The sense of ownness intensifies this, though it is not as incorrigibly individual. Even when I-me and ownness withdraw, as in moments of concentration, and experiences supervene that are no longer merely individual, these are not usually of a nature to demand the word "person". They are rather impersonal. Why? Strange, the word "person", though saying in some way more than "individual" can say, evokes a sense that is rooted in the individual. We can't use the word for anything not based in and on the human individual; other times might, but not today in the English language. Given the history of our words, when we think of the greatest possibilities of the individual human we say, *person.* Not in French or German, not in Greek or Sanskrit, just in English today—with all the riddles and absurdities it brings.

The first of these might be that we don't discover person introspectively in ourselves as we do I and me and self and ownness. There is no universal, self-evident sense of person—as there is of I and me. Person, whatever it might be, is never an object given to be known, not as phenomenon, not as a transphenomenal being. It's discovered through another, though not strictly *in* that other. When something in the eyes, in the face, in the voice of another tells me how much more is possible through a human being than all the virtues of individuality; when some sense of the worth of all things, of the way it must be with life itself is present through another, then I see the furthest reach of the human. I have discovered person.

This compounds the riddle. Sensing the presence of person in a friend or loved one is not like perceiving intelligence or anger or patience in them. It's very odd. Sensing person is not a subject-object event. It's the unwilled, effortless response of one to an effortless, unwilled response in the other. And vice versa. Nothing else could do it. The other is showing the nature of person because he or she is sensing person in me. And I in him or her. Neither wills it or is otherwise aware of it. It takes two and it is between two. Each throws the other back into his or her echo chamber gathering sense of a new depth in humans. One speaks to the speech of the other speaking about one's speech, wordlessly. Each is the source of person for the other. And source is not causal. Person, so presencing, is like an undreamed of truth, a fresh opening of vivial sense, a rare gem, the very substance of human being. So is person discovered. As I know it.

This discovery has not been an I-me-self experience. It's rather that, all variants of I-me and self having been found inadequate, person now has space to show up in. But after the discovery through another person, person may enter any human situation that merits it, unpredictably. And without the mutual recognition essential to its discovery. Don't we treat each other as potential persons most of the time? Unawarely, true, but for that, all the more convincingly? And so person is present in its boundless possibility in the everyday world, indefinably.

Person as Touchstone of Life

So, there is good reason to grasp our own time as a struggle to the death for person. Out of it will come the life sense of the next age. Some, whom one might call naturalists, hold that the human person derives from a cluster of genes and is propelled by psychic complexes toward extinction in a black hole. Its rival, the democratic person, has inherited the ceremonial robes of an earlier time and is seen as a mini-god, describable only in the grandest words we have. He or she is a self-standing, self-determining, reason-endowed, equality-loving person. This very person we then entangle hopelessly in a world of electronically determined "thinking", shallow concepts of freedom, ruthless economic exploitation and political manipulation. The sovereign robes of our democratic person conceal a puppet. The profoundest discoveries about the nature of person from earlier times can't breathe in this polluted air. What has our person as "cultural artifact" to do with Plato's human who carried all truth in himself or with the Buddhist whose own nature was the imperishable nature of Buddha himself? The suffocating everyday is wrapping us in its shroud. Neither the naturalist nor the illusory democratic view has the substance to keep person alive. May the memory of greater thinking stay with us until better times.

As the struggle for person turns out, so will our horizons of vivial sense be drawn. For only person needs vivial sense, and must search for it and live in it. As the range and depth of a person, so the range and depth of his or her life sense. Person is the point of entry of life sense onto the human scene in our time. Any truth reaching us will have to pass through person. A broken melody person may be, but our only musician.

Striking that the ancients saw no need for person on the everyday scene. Vedantists, Buddhists, and Taoists all moved in one step from the everyday individual to his or her source, which after a transformation, replaced the individual: *ātman* replaces the fallacious I-me; *nirvāṇa* replaces the desire-riven individual; and the

Way itself is the immediate reality of the wise person. All are expressions of behavior. They recognize the person potential of the individual human in the concept of the enlightened individual: the bodhisattva of Buddhists, the one emancipated while still living of Vedanta, and the sage or uttermost person of Taoism. So they had no need of the concept of person to rescue individuals. But not so for us! We need person to keep ourselves from being suffocated as artifacts of society or products of nature.

Each of us will use the word "person" to express what each holds to be the potential of the human being. "Person" tells us where to look for and what to do to find our best sense of things. Inner and outer, space, time, words, knowing, opened spaces where something like the mystery of things can be explored. They're touchstones. But they don't convey an adequate sense of the way it might be with all things. They're impersonal. Personal has discovered a further depth in the way life can be for us.

When one no longer sees a nameable social category—mother, brother, employer, friend, male, female, scholar, farmer—in another human, but only unnameable humanness itself, then person is present. The other isn't asking for anything, or trying to manipulate, or help. In such moments face and voice and body simply tell us, without words, of a spirit that is free of deception, of moral judgment, of desire to possess; a spirit that makes us wonder at its utter spontaneity, at its preciousness; a spirit that is beyond the everyday individual without ceasing to be human. Such moments disclose the highest potency of a human being. That is what person can mean to us today. It is its own kind of magic.

Well that's the way person is important to me. A mere sketch. The inexhaustible variations possible even within that sketch! There are the cynics. Relentless in their belief that life is fraudulent, a swindle. And incorruptible. There are the skeptics. Tireless in exposing all beliefs as servants of purposes beyond themselves. Without giving the purpose of their own belief. There are the idealists who trust their own beliefs to be truth. And suffer much from doubt. All are persons—insofar as they have not willed themselves to be what they are, yet accept themselves vivially. So "person" does not name any kind of individual. It's not cognitive. It's a guiding word. It's behavioral.

Person as one's clearest sense of life. That's where I'm at, without intending it. But what happens to the flesh and blood human individual? Does he or she become a person? Or is person one more "inner state" among many? Or is it a vision, a momentary dream? Or an epiphany of truths beyond the human world? Enter the metaphysicians—uninvited. Person is one's sense of life becoming the end of living. But person is not individual. So, how is person related to the individual? It's a paradox of course, not intelligible. But how to take it? Person is not an individual and not an individual trait. Person cannot be discovered in the individual psyche. And person isn't an essential function of the individual, as consciousness and memory are, nor as integral as thinking and willing. Indeed there's a characteristic difference. An individual must be sick if unable to decide what it considers best for itself and to make that the purpose of its will. Person is recognizable by its concern with matters that are beyond human willing. It would be meaningless to say an individual willed his or her sense of the true way of things. That's just what cannot be made the object of an act of will. Vivial sense doesn't speak as a moral ought. When one is moved to embrace a worth outside one's interest or advantage person is present.

But person is not random like lightning. Person can show only in an individual who is ready to give it, if not a home, a resting place. We naturally think of it as an expression of the individual concerned. But on reflection that doesn't satisfy. The individual can have all the faculties of a human being and function without the added powers of a person. As we all do much of the time. A person's acceptance of life is more than an individual attitude or stance, though somehow these do carry over into the quality of the person. Person emerges more as a gift, and certainly quite unwilled. It is latent in every human being. It may presence unobtrusively—mother and child—or it may fill the world—Buddha's enlightenment. That one can't become directly aware of oneself as person, but only in and through another, marks it off from an individual's sense of I-me-ownness. It's not just a contemporary name for the human individual. Person is the most important discovery in the human world. That sound uncomfortably aphoristic. But it's where I'm at.

So back to the question, What is a person? Bad question. Person is not a *what.* "Person", all along and from the beginning, has been not a what word but a guiding word. The initial sense of individual uniqueness lured into further reaches. It led into so many answers: the I-me sense of oneself, the self-aware self, the moral self, the Eastern illusory self, the Western transcendental self. But nowhere did person make if possible for me to say, "Aha, I've found you!" Only by giving up the notion that "person" was a contemporary name for the individual human did it begin to come clear that throughout person had been pointing, not in the direction of personality, but of our best sense of the way of things. And this seemed to be more a gift than an individual achievement.

So "person" is one with inner and outer, space, time, words, and knowing in being a behavior word. Indeed it brings these, fused in their sense, into live situations. Person is present as we are moved to behavior that sustains the worth of life itself. When one's own being must find a new understanding of itself person brings the furthest reach of life sense to bear. Person offers no knowledge and makes no decisions. It is the ambience of sense in which life problems take shape. Life sense is person aware of itself. Person is behavior aware of its vivial bearing.

And it is a word that tells how to treat other humans, not merely how to think of them. It tells that every human being is a being in which a sense of life's worth can come to dwell, if only briefly. So every human being is as precious as that sense of life is. And the worth of life can be in no other way than in a human. That's our destiny—and task. If humans ceased to treat each other as the spontaneous center of life's own sense, could we remain so? Are we alive to the possibility that technological societies, despite high-sounding vocabularies, will constrain their members within an understanding of themselves that precludes a sense of person?

That's grim. But so it should be. How could we survive as what humans have been for millennia without the touchstone of worth that person offers us? If we can nurture a person who is as open as life itself, and only if we can, we may again at some time be capable of believing in a world meant for persons to live in.

VIVIAL SENSE

Exploring Vivial Sense

Person has been saying more than I thought it could. Person has become the way an individual human being is open to the sense of life itself. When we are moved to sustain our sense of life in our behavior we are persons in the furthest reach. This is the thought. This I have come to believe. It makes person heart and hinge of the human world. It seems too much. But that thought arose from the exploration itself. It's not vagrant. Does it make person too powerful? Do we have no sense of life at all except as persons? Well, turn the exploration around and ask what "life" and "life sense" can do for person.

What of the little word "life"? What is its efficacy? Without it I'd be unable to frame many sentences. It's the most embracing word in our language today. Not the span of an individual's existence from birth to death, not the opposite of death, not the kaleidoscope of fresh experiences, not organic nature, not life force. Whatever has been or could be experienced by human beings in whatever form—perception, feeling, knowledge—is life. The experience of other species, so far as that enters the human world through our knowledge of it, is life for the purposes of vivial exploration. Geological and astronomical ages, as we are aware of them, are life. Even what dies to human memory belongs to life through its consequences. It has to be that inclusive. But life isn't the *source* of human experience and its failures. "Life" evokes the mystery humans are born into. Life sense is one way of discovering that mystery—not resolving it.

As a technical term it will arouse indignation. But it has the merit of freeing one's impulse to probe every assumed reality, every science, every belief, every value in every culture we can study. And not just inherited Western philosophical problems. Life is the horizon within which our actions and our ideas find their significance and their worth. Unlike the everyday and the established fields of knowledge, life has no compartments, no barriers, no categorical hierarchy to hinder exploration. It's open to movement on any plane in any direction, though its secrets may be hidden.

Such is the embrace of the word "life". And here I am exploring it. Not as an object but for its sense. And that puts the word "explore" to the test. It says to let flow out. It's not a microscope examination of a dead something but an interaction with what one is exploring so that this reveals itself. When people explore each other's motives—bringing each other's hidden compulsions to the surface, if not all of them—that would be close to it. Probing, with some guiding sense of why one is probing just here and not somewhere else, is exploration. Exploration has to be a move into the unknown.

As vivial explorations want to be: ways of developing a sense of life. However countlessly many such explorations there might be, each will have to be an attempt to find the life worth of whatever one is exploring, from television commercials to mystical affirmations. Any exploration that allows life to be sensed in some aspect is vivial. Vivial exploration can't be an enquiry into unchanging states of affairs, where one is careful not to become involved lest one surrender the prestige of objectivity. Vivial exploration lives with whatever is being explored. Living with implies encountering, reacting to, involvement in. Vivial implies a behavioral aspect to exploring. Not just thinking behavior, but a willingness to reform one's sense of the significance of what is flowing forth in the exploration. It doesn't posit existing substances in the hope of stating theoretical truths about them. It should ask, How do space, time, person . . . speak to me¿ How do they behave¿ How can I make sense of them¿ It should test the worth of one's *own* experience. That's the crux.

Vivial exploration erases the dichotomy of subject and object, even though we are incapable of grasping how. There is power in this conundrum, but it can't invalidate the undertaking. Vivial sense is the highest court of appeal. Nothing can justify or discredit vivial sense, except vivial sense. It's the test of the worth of all experiences, including talk about experience. Vivial sense takes the place of—it's not the same as—terms from an earlier era when philosophers spoke of "truth", "being", "reality", "the absolute", and the like. Vivial sense serves some of the same functions as these, without carrying the same meaning. It's analogous, but without claiming to know how this world looks in God's eyes.

That's a broad statement. And it needs clarifying. Vivial sense has been my workhorse but I've never tried to say what it does for me. It's time I did. No hierarchy of terms; they interweave as one lives them. It is not a definition I want. It's an appropriate range of sense for the expression. Vivial sense is not a faculty of intuition. It's interchangeable with life sense, but is more flexible. Neither vivial nor life should function as concepts. Joining them with "sense" should prevent that possible misuse. "Sense" is a great word and many sided. It is clearly marked off from meaning, definition, inference: everything that can only mislead exploration for our best sense of the way of things. "Sense" says I sense, you sense, someone senses: it evokes concrete experience. It says there is something more to be discovered here. It bespeaks and invites participation. It suggests experiential movement, curiosity. A breath of value sense is integral. And that brings it close to the ways we have of behaving ourselves. Sense is horizontal, not logical; it cannot be reduced to explanatory inference. It is closer to judgment. Not difficult to say all that. I wonder if I adhere to it?

Sense is everywhere, or nearly, it seems. A body movement, a gesture, may of course be a mere signal. But the definable message of a gesture is not its sense. A knowing roll of the eyes has its full significance only for one who is a participant in the situation, who is familiar with the person using his eyes to talk, and with the person or persons so commented on, and with the social purpose of the group and with the intentions and ambitions of its members, and who has a ready keyboard of feelings about all this. An outsider would have no trustworthy sense of the gesture's significance. Sense is participational and presupposes a sensitive behavioral stance on the part of the one claiming to sense what is going on.

The same will hold for words. One hears the meanings of words and sentences, unawarely for the most part. But if one knows the person one is talking with well and is sensitive to what is going on, one can catch the bearing of the words used beyond their meanings and on a range of questions not acknowledged to be integral to the discussion. A disparaging remark about children can remind one of the speaker's attitude to family and genetic engineering. Only one of the family could catch that kind of sense in the remark. Or it might hint at an anarchistic or authoritarian political bent. Roughly infinite, the possibilities.

Sense must be open, always alive with new possibilities. It is not to be defined into a rational scheme of explanatory concepts. It doesn't presume to explain. So it's not another word for intuition. Intuition commonly needs the cognitive model to make sense and is often an easy way out of a cognitive cul de sac. Sense may appear to be that too, but it isn't. Not as I'll have it. Sense and the sensing of sense are one and not to be intelligibly separated in the experience. Sensing is more than becoming aware of the characteristics of a thing or idea. Sensing is awareness of the worth of what is being sensed. Thunder and lightning can have a vivial worth. They speak of the sourceless irrational, of purgatory, of spontaneous life and death. And where there is worth there is behavior. Sense says that knowing and behavior are inseparable, as are subject and object. It's sure that vivial sense is integral to one's behavior. One's sense of the world and one's stance in the world are not separable.

Vivial sense and life sense are a sense for the worth of life. They emphasize the experience more than its content. Vivial will be the significance, the worth of an experience for the discovery of one's sense of life. It's a touchstone so to speak. It's that aspect of something that has worth for all other things. If one is exploring time or the body or language or person, then anything one discovers that tells something about life itself, is vivial. The way life gives itself under exploration for its best sense, is vivial. If I discover that a person is the only being whose behavior can illuminate its own grasp of the sense of things, and whose sense of things can illuminate its behavior—"aware" behavior for me—then that discovery is vivial. And it must be lived. Words can only trivialize it.

Vivial sense doesn't emerge inductively, with proofs attached. And should never claim to be true; no more than philosophic theory can make that claim. Vivial sense is what, in our time, must test the worth of philosophic theories, without the idea of truth.

And it refuses to be spoken of in the same breath as rapture, ecstasy, romantic agony, existential angst, though it senses the life worth in these. Vivial sense arises from experiences that bring the taste of life itself. Any lesser experience, aesthetic, moral or religious, is valid only within its limited field. The moralist, or artist, or religious one, mistakes his or her peculiar sense of worth for vivial sense. Result: dogmatism and intolerance. Vivial sense is the voice of the worth of all things, though it is usually unrecognized as such. This holds for skeptic, cynic, and robber baron when they say, "life is a torment," "life is a rip-off," "life is me first." When anyone attempts to put into words what one's best sense of the way of all things is, one will turn to one's vivial sense as to one's oracle.

Is vivial sense present everywhere? We're aware of it so seldom. What is the vivial sense of a downtown traffic jam, a hospital operating room, TV drama, malice in a friend? The question is impossible, but helpful. No hard, everyday reality carries vivial sense as an attribute. That is what makes the everyday merely real. But in any human situation, if, without an individual's willing it, a significance enters and raises one's awareness beyond the realities of momentary frustration, or fear, or disgust, or hurt and leaves a taste of tolerance or cynicism or wonder that seeps into one's sense of things, then person lives and vivial sense is present. Even though we don't think of it that way.

Vivial sense can presence in any situation, though not in any thing as such. Most often it enters just below articulate awareness, leaves its taste, and disappears again. It can seep through to us over the years, even without our being aware of it. Boredom, dread, self-deception, self-enforced labor are potent sources. That fellow feeling toward the great openness of the night sky or apprehension at the moon waning in amputated helplessness leave their traces. So does the mythic vastness of time past as science makes us aware, or the smile in a friend's eyes that tells of something more than self-will. So does even a new idea when words slip their close-fisted everyday meanings and light up unsuspected fields. Touchstone experiences like these, returning again and again, slowly fuse into a life sense. A clear awareness of one's life sense awaits more powerful jolts. This is a story not often told. But it makes sense.

Vivial sense is not skilled with words. Words cover it over. It begs for recognition as itself, not as the subject of labored prose. Would that I could use Samuel Beckett's language of "nonwords". But nonwords are not no words. They're words used to mock at their own pretensions. Grand thought. But I'm not Beckett. Nonetheless, some probing in forbidden words.

Vivial sense is spontaneous. It moves us; we can't will it, either to come or to go. Spontaneity, awarely lived, *is* vivial. First tautology.

Vivial sense has no use. It's neither inner nor outer. It can't become a means to some end. It has no purpose beyond itself. Nor is anything else a manipulable means to its arising. Second tautology.

It can't be made part of an explanatory system of ideas. It's not related by inference to everyday experience. The everyday can't be related to it by inference. It can't be explained, nor does it explain anything. Third tautology.

It's intrinsic worth. When the worth of a human act is more than moral or religious, when the worth of a poem, or a painting, or music cannot be reduced to poetic or pictorial or musical worth, that worth is vivial. Fourth tautology.

Vivial sense, when awarely present, as it rarely is, reaches to the furthest depths, before it leaves. It is the unsublatable sense of all other worth. It behaves so, without offering any words as explanation. It fulfills itself. To seek to add to it would merely cover it over again. It's not what I thought I was exploring for. So it's the answer to a question that was never asked. Fifth tautology.

Unique it certainly is to each one of us. But not mine, not due to or owned by any individual. It can be only person through whom and for whom vivial sense arises. Sixth tautology.

Enough. What have all the heavy words told me? Can vivial sense be recognized? Is it a value judgment? Is it more than an esoteric name for our most persistent attitudes? Is there any way in which we can know it? If we can't know what our vivial sense tells us, how can we be sure that it is what we believe it to be?

Well, we can be sure. So it is knowable—in some sense. But not in the commonest use of the word. As the great men have said they know something, vivial sense is knowable. It's not an object that the intellect can grasp in a conceptual understanding. Knowing, as I want it, is an exploration by a person. There is no truth that can be expressed in words. A person's vivial sense is not the truth. It's the sense disclosed in aware behavior.

There are good reasons for putting it that way. To look for truth in vivial exploration in an aberration. Truth is truth about something whose existence does not depend on its truth. Truth is the quality of a theory, of a composition of idea words. Truth is kept aloof from lower experiences like feelings, values, decisions. Sense—any sense of situation, word, or gesture—is neither pure idea, nor pure feeling, nor pure value. Let there be undertakings—mathematics, logic—whose terms are definitions within the rules set up for the undertaking, where truth is a function of definitions. In no living situation is this so. The everyday would be for the insane, if it were treated as such an undertaking.

It's the same with one's vivial sense. Only more so. Plato's sense of the irremediable falsity of the everyday world of opinions; Aristotle's sense of an active intellect in humans, the mark of divinity; Chuang Tzu's wandering on the way of all things, free of entanglement in them; Buddha's confidence in an eternal plane of existence waiting for humans; the Vedantist discovery that the self of the cosmos is not different from the self of the person; Nietzsche's conviction that salvation for the human is the acceptance of all things as unchangeably eternal; Wittgenstein's haunting sense that the supernatural is unattainable through any use of the natural world—such is the vivial sense of the great ones. In the West we treat vivial discoveries as theories, to be supported or refuted by argument. But they are not idea complexes removed from a person's experience. They're personal experiences compound of idea, feeling, and sense of worth.

If ideas were entities that lived in a realm into which only ideas, stripped and washed clean of all contaminating feelings and values, were granted admittance, then one could attack or defend these expressions of vivial sense solely with the instrument of ideas. But lived ideas are inseparable from feelings and a sense of worth. They *are* those feelings and values somehow become aware of themselves. Ideas are closest to words, so we retain vivial discoveries in words that initially evoke the idea component of the discovery. But when we try to recapture the full worth of the experience, we have to use the words, not as answers to the puzzle, but as means of exploring the original experience. And they lure and guide us wondrously well.

No more should we lift feelings and worth out of lived sense. The feeling factor speaks only as we say "Seems right" or "I won't have that" or "Opening out" or "Constricting" and so on. A feeling needs the clarity of an idea to be itself. Worth is even less tangible. It is further from, less penetrable by, ideas. But closer to the movement of exploration. Sensed worth of idea feelings is the pulsion that moves exploration in one direction rather than another. But it's not a value judgment. It's the purest spontaneity. The worth seems to be there before we are aware of it. The deep-rooted sense of a Pascal that finds the everyday world corrupted and that discovers another world that isn't.

Vivial sense then doesn't want to be confused with theory, or value judgment, or feeling. It's not exclusively any one of these but the interweave of all. Sensing as such has shown that character. That would put an end to the ancient dichotomy of theory and practice, and so, truth.

The vivial sensing that has emerged so far has all the elements of behavior. So behavior can't be abandoned; it needs to be enlarged. Decisions aren't prominent in vivial experience but affirmation is, and that's one kind of decision. Some will insist that vivial experience may be inner behavior, but nothing more. It is something more. The distinction of inner and outer in matters of behavior is not acceptable. In vivial sensing ideas move as they do in overt behavior: feelings are always present, value preference is continuous, and decisions grow out of this matrix. The absence of overt body action is not essential. In both, all the elements of behavior are present. The word will stay.

How is it that we so seldom become aware of a vivial experience as such? Our common focus on "states of mind", "perceptions", "decisions"—whatever public psychology brings into existence by names—lets us easily forget how static concepts cover over the ceaseless and minute fluidity of all experience. And how they turn our attention away from the inexplicit background awareness that accompanies and carries all our sensing and valuing and deciding. We're seldom aware of the pervasive way we stand to the world, how we feel about ourselves, that is, how we feel about things; and that into this seeps, with unpredictable frequency, a passingly stronger taste of life itself. Soon forgotten, or perhaps not even noted, over time it forms a submerged coral reef of one's sense of things. These passingly aware experiences, having no definable object, may count as vivial in embryo, even though they aren't recognized as that. At night when the thick foliage of the stars wraps the whole world in its effortless strength, and one senses the cosmic fellowship of the night, without saying or even thinking so, that will be a kind of vivial sensing. Or when an innocent cloud arrives from nowhere drifting by on an invisible breeze, and a fresh idea drops in—like an awakening.

And then there are those rare experiences that conspire to bring a strong and aware sense of life itself. That journey to Winnipeg last spring for the class reunion. Two days back in my boyhood world: the streets where we played hockey and fought; my first school; Vernon's house on the corner; the muddy Assinaboine and the caves we dug in its banks to play hooky and smoke our first cigarette in; the old streetcar still swaying its way out to the graves of the parents, Luella, Knox, and Aunt Belle. That entire morning reliving life backward to my earliest memories; and back up again step by step through two wars and all the years until that very moment in the graveyard.

"Vivial sense" sounds cold, almost ridiculous. But the spontaneous continuity of life in the memories. And its free and easy wandering. So easily fecund. No one had planned any of it. Value judgments didn't arise. The parents and family had become as complete and perfect as existence itself. No regrets, no resentments. Just a strange wonder that out of it all, silent little me could come and sit down and feel the oneness in all things, and accept it, and affirm it for myself. Sad it was that death is not as living as life. But not tragic. Death brought life to life. No bitterness. I had come out just about where I belonged, and I belonged with them. In spite of a lifelong conviction I was striking out for distant places.

Vivial sense visited with me that day and carried me willingly along with it. What I believed was happening for me was one with vivial sense; not like it, nor an internal version of it, but the very sense itself. Doing and sensing were no longer distinguishable as outer and inner, or act and content, or however else we might try to describe them. Vivial sense was not an objective truth discovered that day. It was inseparable from a person behaving awarely. It was the aware realization of a life sense. This is the end of metaphysics and all other forms of vivial theory.

There can be no one truth, and no sovereign moral good. Not for me.

All right. But it is now clearer what the expression "person" says. One is a person as one can be moved by a sense of the worth of life: a worth that is without relation to one's own interests or advantage. That is the touchstone. Vivial sense is person turned inside out.

Vivial sense is a way of understanding one's bedrock sense of life. Each person will have a unique version. All of us talk of our own unique life in the language of our own time. Vivial sense is not a persistent "structure" of human life. It's a way of approaching life's abiding incomprehensibility.

If Nietzsche would deign to talk my language, he might say that vivial sense was laying aside the ubiquitous human overlay of good and evil, ugly and beautiful, and rejoicing in the eternal innocence of everything. I can imagine Chuang Tzu saying that there is only one way to discover the Great Way of nature: to disentangle one's private purposes and ambitions from the 10,000 bustling things of the public world and listen quietly to the voice of the greater understanding. And the simplicity of Buddha. He was sure that he wanted release from a world where all things were perishable. His awakening—his realization of the sense of life—was his discovery of the plane of the imperishable. These great ones show the use of the notion of vivial sense. Without that notion we might exhaust our understanding of their quest in the peculiarities of each. But, understood as searching for vivial sense, they stand together in our understanding.

This all seems high up in the clouds. And it is. But vivial sense is also earthy. Are we not creatures of spirit *and* body? It must be so that vivial sense is not reserved for special places and rare occasions. It is the seed sense of all worth. And is always quietly, unawarely on the fringe of consciousness waiting to present with authority, even if unnamed. A person, contorted and contradictory, is still enough of one piece to draw on a sense of the worth of life or lack of worth as needed, even if seldom awarely. One's taste in music, in poetry, in religion, in people, in one's own doings discloses a stable sense of worth. If it doesn't we question the presence of person. A distaste for Baukunst architecture, doctrinal religions and doctrinaire people, narcissistic poetry and music, logically argued philosophy—that is *my* vivial sense protesting. And the preciousness of friends and loved ones and the embrace of a cosmic home is its positive mode.

But our basic attitudes, so much part of our unaware selves we need others to bring them to our awareness? As such they bring no sense of life's way with them. Obviously. But as the basic individual they lend an individual quality to one's vivial sense. When one wakes up and discovers oneself as cynical, nihilistic, adventuresome, closed in, trusting, timid, narcissistic, sadistic, religious—any of these or some others in any interfuse—this will form and color the world that individual is going to live in. As it has been doing from the beginning, unnoticed. The cynic finds the world fraudulent; the nihilist, unworthy; the timid, overpowering; the sadist, hateful. Vivial sense is neither subjective nor objective, neither inner nor outer.

The word "stance" pushes forward again. Of course it explains nothing. It just wants to say that by holding body and attitude together we can see the first faint signs of the individual basis of person. Unfortunately Nietzsche's attempt to derive his "great reason" from the body makes spirit more inexplicable than ever. So does our current popular physiology. Using observable cellular events in one's body as "causes" of one's attitudes and perceptions and mind experiences! That's barbarism. It drops the curtain on human worth before the play has begun. Stance simply makes it possible to avoid metaphysics and to detect in the inexplicable bearing of an individual the first dumb signs of a personal attitude that no individual can have willed for himself or herself but that will shape a person's vivial sense.

And from there the signs lead to fringe feelings, perhaps rare, of a fresh sense of life's possibilities. Occasionally a stronger breakthrough may restructure one's life without it being recognized as an altered life sense. Then more rarely, an awakening to an unanticipated sense of the way it must be with life—vivial sense—mostly without an intelligible account of itself. And of one piece with barely aware fringe feelings and largely unaware life stance. Is that public institution that solves all our problems—the unconscious—useful or obligatory at this point? No, twice. Not that we aren't largely unaware of our own stance. We are. But to derive this stance causally from "the" unconscious is to revert to the ancient ex nihilo dogma. It tells us nothing—except that we are at the limit of our knowledge. Within our experience how can we say more than that a life stance is the embryo of an individual that is potent to discover vivial sense? Because our stance is largely unknown to us, we transfer it and its shaping power to the world, from where it returns to us as if deriving from the world. One's stance is already within the malice or benevolence of the events and people surrounding us every day. And no less is the character of our world already effective in the way we hold ourselves within it. Stance is not toward the world, it shows up in the world, as integral to it. World and stance are mated. They are attuned to each other as inner and outer always are. A cowardly and resentful stance mates with a malevolent world. A naive and brash stance with an adventuresome world. One encounters oneself in every situation, as Nietzsche put it. Stance gives due importance to the unconscious, without expecting an explanation from it.

Vivial sense has just about had its say. But is open to one radical misunderstanding. One might feel that one is fleeing from everyday realities to a beatitude waiting beyond them. That is the naive sense of many experiences of the vivial. But it is not the way life sense is present in the world. To suppose the life worth of things were apart from the things themselves, of another nature, would be the death sentence for the everyday world. It would reduce the everyday to meaningless situation skits one should escape from. It would be transcendence in a bad sense.

It would be. But is bad transcendence the only alternative to bad realism? To deny everyday things all qualities other than those within the realm of causal laws is bad realism. It must cultivate a nihilistic stuffing of the leftovers into the mind and the exclusion of all value from the world. Even as bad transcendentalism must cultivate an equally exclusive narcissism.

Of course these are two extreme stances, seldom realized. Mostly we accommodate some share of both, without being aware of their contradictions. My own vivial sense seems to center in this opposition. Space put an end to the dualism of appearance and reality for me. Emily Carr's abandoned tree is a solid wooden object, so many feet of measured space tall. But its worth was its indominability, which stood out, not in space, but in the boundless. The spatial tree drew nonspatial worth into itself, but only because it was capable of giving it a home. The tree was neither in everyday space, nor yet divorced from it. Or it was both. The logic of contradiction doesn't matter. The way the tree in space discovered nonspatial worth; the way the boundless gave the tree human significance. The absurdity, the unintelligibility of both.

But it's more than absurdity. It's the possibility of vivial sense. Because of its absurdity. It's life's way. To be lived, not explained. To defy our dominant ways of thinking. To be greater than our comprehension. Yet simple and serene, as lived. That is one life sense announcing itself.

That is not a little presumptuous, but so I must have it. Time is no different. Commonly taken as duration, measurable in identical units—seconds, minutes, light years—under exploration, it emerges not as the counting of such units, and not as the element in which events can make sense. The snapshot of myself at about 12, grinning in front of the chicken house I had just whitewashed. That boy is me writing these words. Time isn't sequence, it binds events together. That puzzle is the way of things—for me.

The cycle of the four seasons is no less strange. Autumn follows summer; winter, autumn; and spring, winter—in calendar time. But now and then, perhaps as an early snow abruptly ends autumn, and the thought of winter evokes anticipation of spring gardening, and that leads to a whiff of summer swimming and canoeing—all four seasons are present at the same time. Not as a sequence in time but as a rhythm that transforms the cycle of seasons into a single reality now. Only as seasonal time is there to be transformed, can there be a timeless story of the seasons. Real time and story time are both unintelligible. It's their interdependence that feeds life sense—mine anyway.

Everything can be lived in radically differing ways: as hard reality, as transcendent puzzle, or holding these together, vivially. Words can resound with a sense that was not in the words as heard. Knowledge of an object can metamorphose into a way of living with that object. It's not that two realities—subject and object, inner and outer—though interdependent, remain themselves. It's rather that two seeming realities shed that appearance and become one behavioral experience.

The unceasing transformation of what is inner and what is outer is rich ground for the vivial, and for its misunderstanding. Enjoyment of music and painting and dance and architecture does transmute sounds and sights into experiences of what is not merely heard and seen. But that doesn't ensure its being vivial. Experiences of delight or rapture may be only that. This seems ungrateful, but let me reserve vivial for those experiences that move us with their incomprehensibility. When life opens its depths of wonder and the song or the painting, mere external sounds and sights, so transcend themselves as to move the one enjoying out into the music or the painting and to bring the sounds and sights into the enjoyer as experience. Thus magically coming together in what is neither, nor merely both, but is life, lived. Let that be vivial.

Religion should be an interesting field of vivial experience, but not always is. In the West we seldom experience god as one with ourselves. We won't have it. We want god to be removed and above. That Christian mystics tend to eliminate the otherness of god and their own selves in mystical experience accounts for the little favor they have enjoyed in the Church. The *Cloud of Unknowing* stands alone. The author never gives up struggling to preserve god's incomprehensibility and yet to make his own lowly self worthy of oneness with him. And that makes his account of the struggle vibrantly vivial. He holds to both inner and outer while going beyond them. The central Christian belief that redeeming a human being from nature's corruption is possible only through the unmerited favor of a gracious divinity can itself be seen as a vivial paradox. Sad that the power of religion so often arouses unbending belief in its devotees and not a more open life sense.

Life sense. It remains in the center. One can't be sure how ignorant one is, how floundering one's explorations are. But they're all we have. My vivial sense is rooted in the common realities of this world, I believe. They are the beginning and the opening, I believe. But they make no vivial sense in themselves. Life comes to them as it finds an opening, and things take on a worth that is beyond their everyday nature. Explanations laugh themselves out of court. Only the magic remains.

My colleagues will unwind themselves from their computers and accuse me of deliberately, and not without malice, ignoring the vivial possibilities of scientific experience. Well, it's true, I do carry on as if only certain kinds of preferred experience had vivial possibilities. And that must appear as ignorance or prejudice. Is it?

Well, within a scientific discipline there is only the inanimate reality of laboratories with machines and their data and their hardware and software to keep them working. Of course the scientist's perceptions, conceptual systems, and imagination are there too. But the rules of evidence are untouchable. Where is the spontaneity of life in all this? Can it enter as a calculable factor into experiment or theory? It couldn't, without changing our language. Science is another given, hard reality that, like all such, will, of itself, blanket out its own vivial worth. These are harsh words. But how could it be otherwise? Let the scientists move out of their laboratory behavior world into the nonscientific, noncomputerized areas of sense awaiting them: beginningless history, the spontaneity of all things, the horizonal echoes of words, the riddle of the inner knowing the outer, and the absurdity of ultimate origins. Let them, from this distance, look back on their laboratories and their data bases. Let them see these in their new worth as openings into worlds without laboratories. Let them sense the otherness of scientific method and vivial worth. Let them live the incomprehensible interdependence of the two. And then, let them realize that science is their opening into life sense. Science and computers can be as vivially significant as any other reality behavior.

Fantasy? For our time, almost certainly. Science is the most unyielding reality in our world: harder than sense perceptions, harder than feelings. It covers over the spontaneity of all things. May the fates come to our rescue.

Still, the great empire of the sciences makes one wonder about the validity of indefinable vivial sense. It is so individual, so perspectival. It's like a maple seedling growing in a vast field of machine-groomed wheat. How can it offer itself as a kind of truth? As the only kind vouchsafed us? What of the inherent self-deception of vivial questions and of all ways of answering them? Is vivial sense a miscarriage of sound thinking? No, it's not that, though the doubt is genuine. But vivial sense is not an illusion, not useless. It offers no arguments or proofs because we don't live life in the light of such. We live in the light of our life sense. And this is bedrock experience, beyond the reach of science or logic. Life sense is of course personal. But the sureness of the discovery is adamantine. What could gainsay it?

The Ur-Need for a Sense of the Way of Things

Vivial sense is not a voluntary search that a few odd souls take up. It is the essence of a human. A person is a being who is open to the imperative of living in harmony with his or her sense of life. Each will have a unique sense of the way of life but that doesn't invalidate the notion. It's the innermost, inexpungable nature of the human, not that one can, but that one must live in search of a way of making sense of all things. No matter how unaware this may be or how primitively articulated. It's as involuntary as human consciousness itself. It makes the human human.

It has to be the human ur-need. How else could one find one's way about in this craggy, moiling cosmos where life moves faster than light? It would be an insane world without the innate belief that there was some sense to it all, even if chaos has to make sense. Without such a stable center—the need is the basic stability, not the answer—where would we find the balance to cope with the drift and swell, the peaks and the valleys of the long odyssey? The ur-need is common to all humans, but is capable of infinitely variable fulfillment in persons. One's sense of the way it is with things determines what we can know and no less what we can't. It covers over whatever would be incompatible with itself. A strong sense of the way of things allows one to be the host of circumstance not the passing guest.

To be the host is to be at home. One's sense of the way of all things is as close as a human being can come to an enduring home. Home being where we believe we come from and want to return to. Foxes and groundhogs make their homes in the earth; fish, in water; birds, in the openness of the sky; monkeys, in trees; deer, in the forest; and nomads, in their tents. We humans are nomads that have their home in the best sense they can make of the world. That is the tent we carry with us on our wanderings. Home is the securest haven we know and the greatest amplitude we can have.

That is the lot of us ordinary mortals. But, then, in Greece, or China, or India—and in how many other civilizations?—the ur-need surfaces and humans find themselves in the grip of a live, demanding question bigger than life that will not yield to indifference nor to hurried, habitual, answers.

Parmenides feels the compulsion to pursue the sense of things tirelessly, until he can rest in his answer: Being and Thought are one. Yajanvalkya lives between the earth teeming with individual beings and the heavens of one Brahmanic truth. And he is able to find his home in the sense of things that allows the human spirit and that truth to be no different from one another. Buddha feels enclosed in a world of ignorance and the suffering of being nourished on nothing but transitory pleasures. His ur-need wants to know how to transcend this. He finds his answer in giving up the attempt to satisfy his bottomless desires and living on the plane of the deathless where desires are still. Chuang Tzu has to find his best sense of things in a world of thriving, dying creatures, plants and trees, all encompassed by the eternal rhythms of rejuvenation and rebirth—the way of heaven and earth. His home is to make nature's rhythms the way of his own life.

The notion of ur-need isn't superfluous in understanding these great men. Even if they would find my saying they were in the grip of an ur-need somewhat amusing. It's just that the bilingual oddity says bluntly: there is no point searching for cause or explanation of the human need for a home of life sense. Ur-need says origin, says spontaneous, says unwilled. It says here is an end to metaphysics. Ur-need isn't a phenomenon in consciousness. It simply names the innate human thrust to build a stable sense of how the way of things comes into play. It's not a description. It draws attention to the essential nature of humans as beings who must find some sense in their lives. It's not less than coeval with human life. It's the binding element in all experience.

That expects much from the sense of the way of all things that the ur-need demands. More than from vivial sense, as the awakening realization of the way of life. Vivial sense is the clear awareness of one's taste of life. It holds fast to its touchstone. It is the test of one's sense of the way of all things, which is a telling of vivial sense. It makes sense of it, so to speak. Not as a theory, but as a bridge between one's vivial sense and one's behavioral attitudes.

Plato. The encounter with the idea of the good—his vivial touchstone—is sudden and uttermost. And is the source of his full account of the way he understands things are for humans. His simple story of the pilgrimage of the individual spirit is convincing. That each spirit, before birth into a human body, circles the heavens, viewing the true forms of all things, explains how, when the memory of this truth comes alive after birth humans can devote their lives to recovering at least enough of it to allow them to leave the shadowy cave of the everyday world and re-enter the intelligible world where truth awaits them. It is one of the great stories.

It doesn't offer humans a purpose for their lives, but it does give life a meaning. You can test the worth of what you are doing against an unmoving model written in the starry sky of ideas. The story doesn't serve as explanation or theory, but as a horizon for living. It's an authoritative voice, telling a tale that makes the best sense out of Plato's touchstone vivial experience. We need some such tale to find our way out of the cave.

And not long before, Buddha had lived out the same ur-need in distant India, with strangely different results. It's more difficult to reach the light than in Plato's story. The awakening is buried far deeper. Countless lives. It seems almost too formidable. And there is no prenatal vision to be remembered. Buddha's own story of the long night of meditation, with a vow to die if enlightenment did not arrive, ends in a simple awakening. "The imperishable has been attained," he said. So simple. It's the difference from Plato's more cognitive grasp of his vivial sense that fascinates. Buddha's concern seems to be more to discover the secret of complete mastery of one's life. The crux was to overcome one's craving for perishable things as if they gave life. That is his vivial sense: life offers the imperishable.

What could one say his best sense of the way of things was? About the same as for any ascetic of his time. Each living being suffers through life after life, at each birth bringing the degree of its ignorance or wisdom from previous lives as the basis of its character in the new life. But with lifelong effort and a good teacher, every being can lessen the hold of ignorance. In time one can free oneself entirely and, having no unfulfilled desires, never be born as a human being again: *nirvāṇa.* No objective truths to cognize, just awakening from a false sense of things.

Plato and Buddha bring the ur-need closest to home. In them

it is insatiable hunger that feeds on a cosmic drama. Today the ur-need with its answering sense of things is our only absolute. Truth and being having collapsed. It is the utmost we are capable of. It offers no irremediable answers, only behavioral imperatives. It is a postulate secured in its enactment. It is itself an account of the way of things. The Greeks, the Buddhists, the Vedantists, the Taoists, living in classical ages, could offer dogma to still their ur-need, honestly. But ours is not a classical age. We aren't capable of dogma. It would be a bad metaphysical joke to suppose we had access by some magical words to that abyss of the unknown that lies far out of reach of any language, even of memory.

Is the ur-need to be thought of as differentiated infinitely into individual form? No, that would have no sense. The sense of life that *stills* the ur-need is so differentiated. It must be special to each person for it to have its behavioral relevance. But it makes better sense to think of the need itself as one and common to all humans. That allows us to treat the views of others as relevant to our own. Even of those as far removed as the thinkers in Greece, India, and China. And that's when the sense of life as the defining structure of historically persistent traditions becomes most clear. Buddhist thought has a persistent unity; and so Vedanta, Taoism, and Confucianism. The Greek tradition persists recognizably far into modern Europe. But the contradiction: life sense is individually variable, yet it can take on a form that dominates a culture through millennia. Sounds contradictory, but it can't be.

Early Greek efforts to make sense of the world in mythophysical theories of the cosmos sets the form for a long tradition. Their grasp of life sense as explanation, as theory, still holds for Parmenides, Plato, and Aristotle. However much they criticized one another, they remained within a basic assumption of the singular supremacy of the intellect among human faculties. The supremacy of theory as the way to make sense of things follows. It makes such good sense that it was reborn in modern Europe and persisted without serious question until the time of Nietzsche. And is still our official presumption. So powerful is tradition.

In India Yajanvalkya's vivial search begins from a world in which intense personal discipline was the accepted source of wisdom. His question is of a strikingly different kind than the Greek: how do I realize my destiny as a human? So is the kind of answer he discovers: the individual being is not different from the being and truth of all things; and this can be realized after appropriate personal discipline. He was not expected to establish this as a theory. It's offered as an account of the way of things after the knowledge and explanations of the everyday have been seen through and put aside. His home is not theory, but a way to be. Chuang Tzu and Lao Tzu are as sharply un-Greek as the Indians, in their own way. The Taoist enjoins with his right hand a human life discipline and with his left offers a sketch of the way it is with things themselves. Both hands use the same words. The Taoist true person can distinguish the way of nature from human attempts to interfere with that way. He rises above personal ambition in all social and political affairs, sure that one drop of private interest will breed confusion. As simple and rhythmic and spontaneous and enduring as nature's way, so should be the way of humans. As one's behavior approaches this, one's understanding becomes progressively freed from the confusions of the everyday.

Traditions and Thrall

Putting these traditions side by side makes one simple thought irresistible. Each clusters around two or three pervasive, uncontested presumptions. In India the orthodox Vedantists and the unorthodox Buddhists share the presumption of the behavioral nature of all vivial sense. And the falsity of abstract knowledge. Virtually the same for the Taoists. But the search for sense in classical Greece, which still persists among us, if tottering, stands on its head when put alongside classical Indian and Chinese thought, as this does put alongside Western thinking. Parmenides, Plato, and Aristotle, whatever their differences, are one in the presumption of the supremacy of the intellect, their *nous.* They establish disciplines for the movement of thought from concept to concept, accepting the ability of words to guide the process and express the truth that emerges. They take only one kind of sense seriously: a theory expressed in abstract concepts. Reason is captain of the human soul and the compass of all theory.

The striking difference between the presumptions of Greek-European thought and those of classical India and China justifies the word “tradition”. Logical positivism and Aristotle are in the same tradition: sense is given in theory. Twentieth century Vedanta is as Indian as the Upanishads. Japanese Zen is as Buddhist as Nagarjuna: sense is given in behavior. In each case differences between schools in the same tradition can be understood within the same enabling presumptions. Some things strike you between the eyes.

Whatever might be the external causes of vivial groupings—traditions—persisting through millennia, they wouldn’t touch the unacknowledged presumptions underlying each. What of our latest demon, technology? Can it help? Not obviously. Traditions persist through the most powerful technological revolutions: fourth century B.C. Aristotle and twentieth century Bertrand Russell! And within one technological age great variances of thought are possible: the hard realist Aristotle and the cynic Diogenes! There’s more to it than that. And the way technologies shape our sense of things needs the most intense study. But thrall seems to lie deeper, though not immune to influence.

What could be offered as the origin of a cast of mind lying so far below awareness that it determines not only the kind of vivial sense pursued but what will be accepted as an answer? How account for the strange fact that vivial presumptions are not acknowledged as such by those proceeding from them? For a Vedantist the oneness of the cosmic truth/being with one’s own being is not a presumption but the way one lives. For Descartes rationality as the substance of the human is just as much given. As is a benevolent god. How is it that we don’t recognize our natural beliefs as enabling presumptions on which all further thought depends? How account for the enduring authority of presumptions in a tradition? Mustn’t confuse presumptions with presuppositions. A presupposition must be true if the conclusion based on it is to be true. The two parts are separate, and the relationship is inferential. This is obviously not so for vivial presumptions. Sense of the way of things is not inferential to anything. Its presumptions are not separate from it. They permeate every experience that tests it and they are still present in the life sense itself. No less true for presumptions that favor theory than for those that favor a thought-feeling-value life sense.

This will baffle those who believe that vivial presumptions

must be part of a conceptual system. Still more baffling will be the evident fact that each set of presumptions has the power of a spell over all search for vivial sense—theory or not —within them. A spell holds one captive. And can't be broken except by an impetus from outside. I believe each spell validates its own kind of sense of the way of things. That's a disturbing thought to bring close to traditional philosophy. It speaks of a power that is of another origin than the rational mind. And yet is the decisive element in each tradition. There is no gainsaying it. It descends like a thrall, from no source known to us.

Thrall. At last it comes to word and can throw its light on the strange behavior of traditions. It's been missing from the beginning.

There's no explanation for thrall. How could there be? Thrall is the ultimate "explanation". Better, it offers as much sense as we can expect to find. Thrall is an ultimate surd. From nowhere to the shaping force in history. The rational historian is outraged. But why should human history not be a surd, when each individual life must be? Why lock the mystery away in our computers? Let's free it, to be our revered habitat.

Thrall. A profound enlightenment that holds captive. But who, or what, is enthralled? It's clear that it makes no sense to say that it is the ur-need. The ur-need must remain outside of historical limitations. Or human existence will become not merely a mysterious surd, but irredeemably corrupted, a causal chain. Again, it can't be the individual answer to the ur-need that is in thrall. Everyone's best sense of the way of things determined from the beginning by a hidden power? That would reduce the pursuit of life sense to a mockery. Unthinkable. There remains only what lies between the universal ur-need and individual sense of things: the *way* an individual pursues the sense of things, and the *kind* of sense that an individual will accept. The difference between Socrates and Buddha. That completes the circle: it is the tradition that is in thrall, that introduces direction, prejudice, and enlightenment to the individual attempt to fulfill the ur-need. There are no arguments for that. It's just that no other account makes acceptable sense.

Thrall is enabling presumption but not a mere starting nudge. It accompanies and permeates all judgments of sense that arise within it. It is inescapable. The lifelong pursuit of the sense of things is enthralled in two senses of the word. It is captive, though unaware of its captivity; and it moves with sovereign confidence through all conundrums. If one's sense of the way of life binds all experience—non-sense, truth, fury, creative passion, stupidity, cruelty, boredom, rapture, whatever there is—together in a livable way, then thrall is the shape and the bond of that way.

That says that thrall is the possibility of meaningful living. Without thrall one would never know how to set about making sense of life. Thrall shapes the pursuit of sense and guides its adventures. There has to be something like thrall—call it by any name—that can enable the personal human adventure to commence and that bears it along throughout its career. Thrall would be mistaken as ideology, or superstition, or religious dogma, or philosophy. Thrall is what enables each of these to make sense—to those espousing them. It is the hidden horizon from which vivial sense returns as echo. Thrall is not a fault to be removed. It's the source of whatever light may rest on one's sense of the way of things. It is itself never grounded, yet it is the unspoken ground of the sense that it enables within itself. It we acknowledged vivial circles thrall would be the paradigm of such.

Yet, thralls aren't forever. They lose their power and dissolve in time. They may encounter other, incompatible thralls equally powerful, each forcing the others to disclose themselves as what they have been all along. That's what the classical thralls of two or three millennia are doing to each other right now. The Indians and Chinese are already more open than we, but the encounter is just beginning. We are at that time in the span of a thrall when the cultures dependent on it are in decline and vivial exploration, now aware of other traditions, is freed to penetrate to the roots of the breakdown. As a thrall is laboriously brought out into the light it must lose its power: to grasp a thrall as an ungrounded presumption is to destroy it. It's sure we're moving into a time when the Western enthralment to theory—science now—is surfacing because life within that enthralment is beginning to destroy itself.

At the risk of being presumptuous, may it be that other classical thralls will surface in our time and compel their cultures to find fresh versions of their traditional beliefs? Is "truth" as a faith not endangered everywhere? Will not even Buddhism and Vedanta have to relinquish the *truth* of their dogmas in favor of a grounding in vivial sense¿ Will not all peoples be compelled to discover new ways of being human¿

Thralls East and West

Thrall and sense of the way of things can't be defined. They intertwine hopelessly. They are indispensable, guiding notions but not to be used for metaphysical theory. Thralls are clearly unconscious, but are neither Freudian nor Jungian. They're not unconscious psychic determinants of personal experience. They lie much deeper than that. But they're not universal archetypes either. They arise and perish in time. They are a special kind of ignorance—vivial ignorance. Thrall says we are naturally unaware of the origin of our ways of grasping and behaving with things. There seems no hope that vivial sense can be transparent to itself. Thrall helps understand how cultural traditions can have the power they have on the human scene. In our day science is a striking instance. It usurps all right to determine the nature of things: water *is* H_2O. Not the source of life on earth, nor the mirror of heaven's imperturbability. Thrall allows us to see the limited potentiality of the philosophical urge and of all other vivial adventures. Thrall is a basis for understanding all traditions within one common human enterprise.

Words, words, words. Easy to thread into necklaces and baubles. And yet. How else preserve what we learn from unearthing traditions¿ Why study past enthralments if they are dead history¿ They aren't, of course. But what to do with disinterred thralls¿ They're not for reburial in the archives. They are our wisdom. Their very failure allows us to catch an enthralling glimpse of the eternal human need to give some deep sense to life, and of what might be beyond life that thrall prevents us from experiencing. They're our hope for whatever future human beings may have. This thought is itself enthralled and may be a dangerous presumption. But I can't see it otherwise.

So thralls are more than the structure of tradition. Disinterred, they tell a wonderful story. We *see* how the ur-need takes shape as dreams that never can become real. The Greek dream of a rational human world in a divinely rational cosmos; the Vedantic dream of a life lived in oneness with the eternal truth; the Buddhist dream of an enlightened life joined with all things by an imperishable compassion; the Taoist dream of a life become one with the ways of nature. Each an answer to the ur-need. But each is only partial because formed by enthralment. Enthralment throws up a grand paradox. Even as dreams fade, the enthralment in each lights up what it was that the unenthralled ur-need was in need of, and failed to find. It's from the fading of the dream that we can learn.

Dethralling traditions is not a parlor game. It's bedeviled by the simple fact that what is truth under one thrall is heresy under another; and by the way thralls sink their roots in the behavioral strata of those enthralled. It's not from ideas alone that thralls have their millennial staying power.

Plato and Aristotle could not believe otherwise than that the best sense of the way of things took the form of reasoned knowledge, that the clearer and more definable we make our ideas, the nearer we approach the truth of being. Pyrrho's skepticism and Diogenes' cynicism made them outcasts. Aquinas was sure he could demonstrate all of god's attributes, excepting only his quality of mercy. Descartes' clear and distinct ideas, and the empiricism of the British thinkers, perpetuated the primacy of knowledge. Odd that Kant's laborious attempt to limit knowledge to matters of space and time had the effect of focusing attention on the reality of science. Even Hegel's mighty effort to encompass all knowledge in a superior wisdom failed to alter the movement toward the exclusive epistemic rights of scientific "fact"; that is, the exclusive existence of the natural world. Inevitable that, as the sciences swelled and philosophy faltered, the modern notion of knowledge should close tightly down to theories that could be tested in controlled laboratory experiment. Not in the fullness of living as Nietzsche demanded. Little wonder that our philosophers continue, with enthralled complacency, to look down on the thought literature of other traditions as not being truly thought literature at all.

The irony of provincialism. In their turn the despised non-Greeks put down the spinning of philosophical theories as the occupation of the unenlightened and the theories themselves as ignorance. What else? Their understanding of the human predicament demanded emancipation from the hegemony of the cognitive intellect. How could they search for a reasoned ground of the sense of things? A Buddhist couldn't prove the truth of the Buddha nature in all things. It's the Buddha nature in oneself that makes it possible for one to discover the Buddha nature in others. Clear. A Vedantist couldn't attempt to give reasoned grounds for the existence of *Brahman,* because *Brahman* is the immanent light in persons that makes reasoning possible in the first place. The Taoist would be the least pervious to reason. Single words with fixed meanings, reasoned or not, could have no access to the *tao.* Only by behaving as the *tao* itself behaves could one discover it. Each of these traditions would have found any attempt to secure it by reasoned argument upsidedown ignorance. Whose is the heresy?

Looking into the provenance of one's sense of the way of things disturbs complacency. Enthralment rises up from its hiding place and bestrides the way of vivial exploration like a colossus. It removes any base of truth. Life sense, philosophical or other, is no longer incorrigible. It's more like a view of things seen in a curved mirror. The rightness of one's view, become a life stance, is confirmed by the distorted image. Yet the life stance itself brings the curve of conviction, a curve that remains unknown to the viewer. So my mirror tells me! It can become evident only to someone whose mirror has a different curve. That means no sense of the way of things can be true. Its authority holds only until surpassed. More. No human experience can every be fully transparent to itself. Sounds gloomier than Pascal.

Vivial Sense and the Sense of the Way of Things

But it's not the last word. What is the life view seen in the curved mirror? Of course it's the home of sense that the ur-need has brought to life, but how do I take that? As the spontaneous realization: this is the very way, the very savour of life itself, one's vivial sense? Or as the more articulate sense of the way it is with all things; that is, the way one takes life? These two experiences are interwoven, but the difference is enough to make it better to hold them apart. Inseparable as they are.

Vivial sense is the hearth of one's home so to speak, but not the whole of it. It's the well one returns to for water but not the life it sustains. It's the diamond that cuts other stones into pattern. It's the heart of one's best sense of things. My vivial sense holds to the way apparent opposites together bring life into our experience: space and the boundless, time and the timeless. So incomprehensible it merits only one word: magic. It comes and goes of itself, beyond any explanation.

But it's not the full story. And that is just what one's best sense of the way of things tries to be. My best sense—so it seems—is a narrative account. It begins with the inborn ur-need. Vivial experiences are the bedrock clues around which I've slowly fashioned a story. It's clear in the story that the human life world bounds our understanding, but that it is not itself understandable. There must be a source of the ur-need and of the answering sense that penetrates the human world in vivial experiences. The source discloses itself, well disguised, in the awareness that the human life world is a mystery. To be aware of mystery is to be aware of more than mystery. That more is a trace of the source.

Aristotle is a prime illustration. His touchstone experience must have been the purity of the spontaneous mind when thinking becomes aware of itself thinking. His account of the way it is with all things pivots on this discovery. Aristotle would have a divine being, god, whose very nature is understood in terms of the human vivial experience: pure thought thinking pure thought. God is unmoved himself but is the source of the motion in matter that allows it to take on the forms of the myriad things in the actual world. The highest achievement of humans is to realize the divine purity of thought. No one trusted the power of argument more than Aristotle.

How are touchstone experience and the account of it related? It's clear that without vivial experience there would be no story of the way of things to tell. But without the story the experience would remain an oddity. It gains its credibility and its worth from the telling of how it can be. The two interpenetrate. So one's sense of the way of things can't be a causal explanation. The reasoning of Aristotle and Descartes is obviously circular. It's better to say that one's vivial experience and one's account of the way of things strengthen one another. They are not separable. The experience gains its authority from the account; and the account, its substance from the experience. Each allows the other to become what it is.

Striking how strongly behavioral one's sense of the way of

things is. Even Aristotle's pure thought is his supreme good. It's something like myth. It allows one to test the worth of an experience against a model written in the stars. It binds the contradictions and incomprehensibilities of life into a drama worth living out. It's not a drama of life and death. It's a drama in that the outcome can't be foreseen and it moves oneself into the center, as hero or antihero. A sense of the way of things tells us that we can do what our vivial experience demands of us. It's not a Kantian imperative. It is, inexplicably, our highest authority and yet leaves us free to live up to it or not. It's more like a horizon of worth within which we come to know if we are the person we believe we can be.

So the ur-need is in want of a home of sense whose light and warmth come from vivial experiences and whose frame and roof are one's sense of the way of all things.

Nietzsche

This is so antitheoretical, so antiintellectual many will hold it to be outside the Western tradition. Outside of modern Western philosophy it certainly is. But not outside the Western counterculture suppressed for so long. Not only by philosophers, but by science, by orthodox religion. Its time has come. Cultural disintegration and proliferation certainly offer it an opening. It already has a prophet and a symbol in Friedrich Nietzsche.

It's increasingly clear that Nietzsche is the new beginning in the Western vivial tradition. His attack on the supremacy of theory as vivial sense is ferocious. He's more than a turning point, he's a fresh start. Once again a human who could place himself in the service of exploring life. And who knew that as life was lived so it made sense. Even though academicians have treated him as an outlaw, the depth of his revolution is making more and more sense. The paradox is that Nietzsche knew little of Sanskrit texts, even in translation, and virtually nothing of Chinese. Yet he spent his life—giving it, literally—undermining the presumptions of European thought and so, not quite intentionally, opening the way to other vivial traditions.

As the first European academic to fight the most deeply buried, and the most obvious, of all Western vivial presumptions: that the intellect, by itself, grasps the truth of all things in conceptual theory, Nietzsche's importance is singular. As for many ancients in India and China, for him the intellect is a life faculty, not a theoretical faculty. Nietzsche is the first Western thinker to make life his central problem. He's an explorer of life, a vivial thinker. That's the key to it all.

He tells us himself what his touchstone of vivial sense is: the power of an idea pulsing through the mind. This pulsion of power, Nietzsche believes, arrives through and from the body—from the lived body, not the mere flesh. Nietzsche's body is the source of life. But he is no biological determinist. He is adamant: the life of the intellect in its search for truth as in its pronouncements on good and evil is, must be, only the powerful will of life itself finding creative expression. His attack on an intellect that gives itself its own laws is unrelenting. He lives his deepest thoughts as arising from his "entrails". His inner depths, as I read him.

His vivial sense is more explicit than in any previous European thinker and unfailingly of poetic power and contradiction. Life is the creative power by which each species establishes an enclave for itself in the pulsating cosmos. Turtles develop hard shells: philosophers, hard truth. The inexhaustible spontaneity of this creative power—that is Nietzsche's life sense. When one thinks of the philosophical and religious dogmas he had to overcome to be sure of this! Herculean. As was the overcoming of his own suffering and nihilism in order to embrace whatever life brought him.

He refuses to be a school philosopher offering rational arguments for the truth of his views. Mostly he succeeds. But in some places the ancient habit of forming theories does slip under his guard. He offers reasons—a universe of infinite time in finite space—for his story of the eternal return of all things: that everything that could happen has happened innumerable times in the past and will happen ceaselessly in the future. He would have been more true to his own convictions if he had stuck to his belief that the acceptance of the eternal return of all things is a test of a human's ability to live courageously in a coming age of wasteland nihilism and the only way to live the paradox of the perishable and the imperishable. That was its worth for him: eternity as the basic notion of the way it is with life. That little poem with the refrain "I love thee, oh eternity" is the most persuasive telling of his story. Then the simple line "Every thing has been baptized in the well of eternity". That's my essential Nietzsche. And the orthodox find it a mess of irrelevant passion, in doubtful taste.

"Loving one's fate": accepting all of one's past life as beyond reshaping by one's own will, fills out the story. And yet, no one has allowed the human person more power to alter the course of history than Nietzsche. One's salvation from a degenerate European culture already heading into an era of nihilism is in one's own power, no one else's. His "eternity" says that every moment of life is infinitely precious. If one can live that belief, one becomes a revolutionary. The lover of fate is still a creative individualist. The problem is to learn not merely to say "yes" to all things, but to act out that "yes" as one lives.

What do I learn from Nietzsche? Not quite everything. But much.

He introduced the word *life* into European thought and made it the term carrying the heaviest weight of worth and sense in his vocabulary.

He sees knowing and theory not in a field of truth, but in a field of behavior. Truth is not the mark and guarantor of knowledge, but whatever serves the life potential of the one believing it. All his key ideas—eternity, love of fate, remaking the human being, accepting the preciousness of all things—are ideas to be lived, not merely thought. They probe into the sense of life itself. They are Nietzsche's own best sense of the way of all things.

He is more than postmodern. He is post-postmodern. He bursts the epistemic bounds of language. He understands that words can reach the unworded through behavior. He grinds sacred truths not into powder but into grist for a coming era that will desperately need new ways of being human.

All that. And in spite of the excesses and contradictions of his work. Which one need not accept. And in spite of his human capacity for self-deception. Still, it was one of his Christian friends who could say "I felt spiritually freer in Nietzsche's presence than with anyone else ever." And then Heidegger, strengthening Nietzsche's work by showing how thinking is not an isolated performance of the intellect. Nor a cognitive undertaking.

Science

That all makes vivial exploration appear too much an individual enterprise. It is that, true. But individuals do not develop a need for life sense ab initio. Their time and society and specific tradition offer basic elements. Buddha's assumption of the truth of rebirth is difficult for most of us today, though Buddhism would have been unthinkable without it. Plato's prenatal space flight depends on the existence of the individual soul apart from the body—for many a poetic tale. Immutable physical laws of space and time were inescapable in Nietzsche's day, so he had to find the possibility of salvation in the nature of the human person. And ourselves. Science has seeped into our understanding of the world and our feelings about ourselves far more than in Nietzsche's time. It is the self-evident basis of truth in any psychological, social, or cosmological argument. It offers itself as a sense of the way of all things. Our sciences have established an accidental and meaningless "beginning" of our universe in nuclear combustion. They describe the slow emergence of living matter and its forming into beings of many species under the sovereignty of genetic determination and environmental accident. They tell of the recent appearance of a two-legged, upright creature with a larger central nervous system than any other species and so the ruler of all beings in a physical world of immutable laws, or immutable chaos, that all of us may not understand, but must nonetheless bow to in deference.

A solemn and impressive story. But not an acceptable account of the way things are for humans. Held against Plato, Buddha, Nietzsche, something is awry. Science's world is not a world that offers a human being the right to live his or her life as a drama worth living. How is it that most of us don't sense the scientific world as an absurdity, as a perversity, as an inhuman conception? Because we must do so if we take it literally as the whole story. Somehow we defend ourselves against it. We all, laboratory scientists included, have vivial beliefs that so far have survived science. Do we not all have a sense of individuality, even of person when we talk of freedom or the sacred right of individuals to fulfill themselves in their own way? Isn't that the seed thought of our social concept and of the way we understand ourselves?

So, our common sense of the human world is not only outside

of the scientific world, but in conflict with it. Free persons are not scientifically discoverable, and vivial persons are not scientifically mentionable. Of course if person became merely a unique being, and freedom merely the right to follow one's inclinations, then laboratory psychology could ingest them comfortably. In such event some new defense would have to tell us that science cannot be lived. Where is the life drama in computer data?

Sense of the Way of Things as Life Drama

Life drama is so pretentious. It needn't be written by Shakespeare. It needn't be Augustine's struggle toward the light of the Christian truth against the vicious drag of his body pleasures, nor the struggle of the Good Lord with Satan for possession of John Bunyan's soul. It needn't be Faust, so thirsting for the beautiful and the true that he sells his soul to the devil. Although there is a frightening truth in that. It needn't be Nietzsche, so driven to strip off falsity and hypocrisy from his impulses and feelings that he sold his sanity in the struggle. It may be just a battle against failure or against the ease of losing before the battle begins. It may be the battle of the marketplace: success equals self-realization. For us today the underlying drama is the challenge to realize oneself as a person, in a world that would sell us inexpensive surrogates. In whatever form, vivial sense is merciless. It unerringly tells you how you have passed your life this time around. As if I knew!

Is that a kind of metaphysics? Not by intention. It says, for myself, that one cannot explore much further along one's vivial trajectory than the worth of life drama. It's a kind of resting place. Like a metaphysical theory. Except that in metaphysics it's the intellect that comes to rest, in vivial exploration it's the person. Both assure us that our cosmos is home to human aspirations. Both allow a fit destiny to humans, if not always a happy one. But the difference. Metaphysics describes its resting place in a conceptual theory. The mind alone has been behaving, its ideas riding on unacknowledged value preferences. A vivial story is also behavioral, but is primarily value preferences riding on virtually invisible ideas. It engages as much of a person as can be, through a story whose every move we must live for ourselves. We test its worth by enacting it. The stories told by Plato, Buddha, and Nietzsche are authoritative because we can enact them. The person is more wholly engaged in vivial story than in theory. A radical difference. With revolutionary possibilities.

Further. In a drama of which one is the hero, or antihero, one accepts vivial responsibility for oneself. Not just for one's acts or decisions. For oneself, for the kind of person one is. We do this naturally, without genetic theory and without any need for the rebirth story. To accept oneself as one's own responsibility defies cause and effect explanation. That's clear. It's a mark of respect for person. Could we be persons and think of ourselves as the objects of mindless fate? Rocks vomited up by the volcanoes of history? That would be an intolerable absurdity. Person cannot be lived as an object. Yet not everything vivial is person. In the vivial drama there is a pervasive ambiance of sense—a gift—from which the worth of the drama derives. No person generates that.

Source

Then, under a full January moon, two clear thoughts. What sense of things reaches me from the night? The simple answer: buoyancy, many splendored, infinite, a haven, a gift. And, what sense reaches me from myself? From a being who must seek the sense of its own need to make sense of its quest for the sense of all things? No answer.

No answer? But of course. The substance of such an answer could never be lived in aware behavior. Could never be experienced vivially.

And yet. Not a bootless question. Unanswerable, certainly. But asking pressingly if positive vivial experience is the end term. If life is a field of experience enclosed in an unscalable wall? Is that all the explorations of person and time and space could tell me? Can I dismiss the paradox of a space that is not spatial, of a time that is timeless, of a person that is more than an individual as the blunt fact of incomprehensibility? Each is that, indeed. But does incomprehensible paradox, lying on the horizon of my search for some sense in the way of things, exhaust the worth of the exploration that discovers it? Does it tell all there is to tell about a vivially receptive person who is impossible without a perishable material body? Why do I think now that there is more in that discovery than mere paradox? Why do I want to say *mystery?*

Because mystery brings with it a sense that is absent in its very presence. Mystery is more than evident incomprehensibility. It says something lies behind the limits of life exploration. It can't be a deadend term. A sense of this lingered on the fringe of the exploration of person and of each of the other explorations. Something was missing. It seems now that mystery was missing. Better, an appreciation of how much more "mystery" says than "paradox". Mystery arrives hinting that it has come from some other where. Clearly it can't open itself and remain mystery. Yet it has the confident manner of something concealing more than it reveals.

Does this mean that the ur-need was more ambitious than it had the right to be? Well, perhaps. But again, it justifies its unspoken promise by impelling vivial exploration to the limits of experience and there allowing it the merest hint of something beyond those limits. It makes sense so. The quest for a sense of the way of life is itself behavior. Behavior can understand itself only as within a world that accepts it and affirms it and allows it fulfillment. When the world refuses to do that, we run aground. But mysteries that hint at their absent source do not bring shipwreck. They don't end the voyage. They make it real rather. They justify and fulfill the behavior that discovered them.

So the ur-need doesn't deceive us—though we may misread it and expect what cannot be. There is no vivial experience of what may lie beyond human experience. Mysteries are all we have. But they and their source are not idea ventures. They are sustained by our behavior in moments of severest crisis and greatest freedom. Is there another criterion?

So. My enthralments have done their best, and worst. May it be as Lao Tzu said: "Roots grow deepest when the trunk is fenced around."

NAME INDEX

Aristotle, 63, 85, 101, 157, 175
Augustine, 40, 116, 124

Beckett, Samuel, 68, 156
Buddha, aware behavior, 139; enlightenment, 128–9; knowing, 103; time, 48, 63; ur-need, 167; vivial sense, 157, 160, 168

Carr, Emily, 28, 33, 162
Chuang Tzu, aware behavior, 141–2; knowing, 98; language, 82, 142; vivial sense, 77, 167, 170

Debussy, 27
Descartes, 16, 101, 104, 117, 171
Dewey, John, 99, 101
Dignaga, 71

Freud, 129

Galileo, 24

Hegel, 59, 64, 175
Heidegger, 40, 44, 51, 69, 84, 180
Herder, 69
Husserl, 44, 85

James, William, 99
Jung, Carl, 142

Kant, Immanuel, 23, 64, 74, 116, 129, 143, 175
Kierkegaard, 51, 59, 75

Lao Tzu, 83, 98, 141, 170

Nagarjuna, predication, 82; space, 15, 23; truth, 73; words, 91
Newton, Isaac, 16, 101, 104, 142
Nietzsche, body, 129–30, 133; falsity, 45, 54, 71; great reason, 76, 140, 161; knowledge, 99, 102; non–knowledge, 79, 82, 85, 93, 95–6; life sense, 80, 103, 104, 160; vivial thinker, 178–80

Parmenides, 167
Pascal, 81, 158, 176
Plato, aware behavior, 139; knowing, 97, 100; person, 144; time, 63, 64; vivial sense, 157, 167–8, 175

Rousseau, 5

Sartre, 51
Shankara, 97, 117
Socrates, 52, 127

Thoreau, 63
Thomson, Tom, 28, 33

Wittgenstein, 86, 93, 157
Wordsworth, 63

Yajnavalkya, 48, 94, 128, 167, 169

Zeno, 15, 18

SUBJECT INDEX

Belief, 5, 6, 20, 65, 93, 94
Behavior, aware, 137–143; enlightenment and, 129; knowing and, 91–3, 97–100, 109, 110; Nietzsche, 180; person and, 151; vivial sense and, 60, 154, 158, 177–8, 184; words and, 70–74, 81, 84
Bhagavad Gita, 58
Brahman, see Vedanta
Buddhism, space, 17, 28; time, 41, 48, 49; words, 69, 72, 73; knowing, 95, 98–9; person, 124, 129, 147, 148; life sense, 175, 176

China, 50, 52, 67, 141, 173
Christian, Christianity, 33, 90, 114, 116, 124, 129, 141, 164
Communication, 13, 68, 69
Confucian, 41, 50

Enlightenment, 129, 143
Everyday, the, inner and outer and, 2, 3, 4, 7; knowing and, 87, 88, 89, 93, 97; space and, 25, 27, 29, 30, 32, 35; time and, 41, 62, 65; vivial sense and, 155, 156; words and, 67–70, 77

Feeling, inner and outer and, 5, 7, 9, 13; space and, 16, 26; vivial sense and, 157, 158
Freedom, knowing and, 110, 113; person and, 125–7; source and, 184

Gnosticism, 95, 128
Greece, 33, 84, 85, 90, 127, 128, 174–5

Habitat, 8, 40, 82, 172

I, 3, 4, 7, 87; freedom and, 124–7; phantom as, 121–4; sense of, 117–9
Idea, 5, 7, 26, 157
Idealist, 4, 16, 33, 74
Ignorance, 143
Illusion, 32, 82
India, 27, 41, 48, 67, 94, 128, 169, 173
Individual, the, 1, 125–6; person and, 143–6, 149, 161
Inner and outer, behavior unites, 12; everyday not disjoined into, 2, 3; knowing and, 85, 86, 90, 91, 105–6, 108–9; paradox and mystery, 11, 13; person and, 144; space and, 9, 10, 15, 16, 19–20, 29–30; subject and object not, 5; vivial sense and, 30, 31, 35, 161, 163–4; words and, 70
Islam, 28, 39

Knowing, family of, 94–96; gnosis, 95; inner and outer, 85, 86, 90, 91, 105–6, 108–9; intellect and, 90, 93, 101, 102; names and, 87; Nietzsche, 99, 103–4, person and, 110–11, 156; philosophy and, 94; rationality and, 104–7; reality and, 89, 92–3; technology and, 109; truth, 98, 108–9; uniqueness of, 90; vicious circle of, 91; words and, 85, 92

Life, 11, 77, 78, 82, 133, 151–2, 163, 179–80

Magic, 35, 45, 82, 137, 148, 164, 177
Mask, 35, 65, 67, 71, 79, 113
Me, 3, 7; phantom as, 121–4; sense of, 119–121
Metaphor, 12, 19, 97, 123
Metaphysics, 3, 4, 16, 160, 167, 182
Mystery, 11, 69, 177, 184
Myth, 13, 127, 178

Nihilism, 108, 162, 180
Nirvāṇa, 49, 110, 129, 142, 148, 168

Object, objective, 1, 5, 10, 18, 53, 152, 156, 161

Paradox, 2, 13, 82, 86, 139, 149, 183
Pathetic fallacy, 30, 31–3
Person, 81, 83, 110, 111, 149–50; battleground as, 114; behavior aware, 137–43; body–mind and, 132; cultural artifact as, 147; discovery of, 146; freedom, 124–27; guiding word as, 149–50; individual more than, 145; Kant, 133–36; magic as, 148; Nietzsche, 129–30; own, sense of, 136–7; self, 127–9; soul-psyche as, 116; vivial sense and, 151, 154, 156–7, 159–60, 166, 183; world and, 150
Positivism, 68, 69
Post modern, 68, 85
Pragmatism, 75, 99–100

Realism, realist, 1–5, 11, 15, 16, 18, 26, 37, 67, 73
Reality, 126, 152; inner and outer and, 1, 5, 7, 8, 11, 12; space and, 15, 18, 30, 35; time and, 39, 40, 43, 46; words and, 70, 71, 82; knowing and, 90–3, 102, 108
Reason, 81; intellect, 90, 93, 101, 102, 105, 156, 170, 178, 179; rationality, 102, 104–7, 130, 135

Science, 1, 4, 7–8, 11, 13, 26, 181–2; western, 96, 100–02, 104–09, 114, 165
Sense, 2, 15, 42, 75, 76, 80–4, 110, 153, 154; of life, 8–10, 15, 26, 27, 57, 59, 60, 62, 64, 79, 81, 94, 104, 145, 147, 149, 150, 152–3, 163, 169; life drama as, 182–3; of way of all things, 16, 83, 166–8, 175–8
Semiotics, 27, 77, 79
Space, spatial, 2, 10, 12, 14–36; cultural, 19, 26; distance or extension not, 21; individual, 27; openness as, 31; physical as, 17, 18, 32; possibility of movement as, 23, 24; postulate of behaviour as, 23; reality as, 15; value attributes and "spatial" objects, 32, 34; without structure, 22
Source, 57, 76, 84, 109, 126, 151, 177, 183–4
Stance, 143, 161–2
Subject, subjective, 1, 5, 6, 54, 152, 161; object and, 1, 81, 152

Tao, see Way, the
Taoism, Taoist, 72, 95, 98, 101, 103, 105, 114, 124, 131, 147–8, 174
Technology, 9, 26, 101–2, 107, 109, 114, 171
Theory, 8, 11, 16, 86, 99, 104, 157, 169–70, 180
Thrall, 172–6
Time, experience not in the "now", 55, 58; habitat as, 40; iz, waz, to-be, 42–7; modes of as fields of behavior, 47–55; possibility of a lifestory as, 64; possibility of a sense of life as, 64, 65
Tradition, 169–72, 174–5
Transparence, 13, 55, 84, 139
Truth, behavior and, 20, 72–3, 98; Buddhism in, 168, 173–4; dogma and, 160, 169; everyday and the, 105, 108; Nietzsche, 79, 82, 99,

103, 180; philosophy and, 153; science and, 13, 105, 108, 109; Upanishads in the, 34, 84, 94, 128, 167; vivial sense and, 154, 156–7, 158, 159, 173–4; words and, 72–3, 85, 113

Upanishads, body, 131; knowing, 94; language, 84; self, 128; sense, 76–7; space, 20, 26, 34; time, 48

Values, 16, 32, 33, 133
Vedanta, behavior, 100, 171; body, 133; *Brahman*, 48, 49, 96, 124–5, 176; knowing, 102; person, 146–7, 157; truth, 72–3, 173–4
Vivial exploration, 16–7, 26, 42, 46, 57, 69, 81, 113, 115, 139, 149–50, 152–3, 157, 181, 182, 183–4
Vivial sense: also see Worth: behavior and, 81, 104, 152, 154; everyday the and, 155, 162, 164; human experience, not beyond, 184; person and, 147, 149, 150, 182–3; sense of the way of things and, 176–8; six tautologies the, 156; subjective or objective not, 161; time and, 42, 49; truth the, not, 157, 159; words and, 155

Way, the, 49, 96, 110, 131, 148, 160; *tao*, 49, 142, 176
Western, 49, 62, 90, 93, 128, 164, 170, 173; see also Science, western
Words, 67–84; behavior and, 46, 47, 50, 51, 52, 53, 55, 84, 92; cognitive primarily, not, 76; echoes and, 77, 78, 83; guides as, 15, 55, 59, 65, 74, 84; knowing and, 85, 91–2; limits of, 84; masks as, 31, 35, 41, 67, 71, 79; meaning and, 68, 69, 78, 81; necessary illusion as, 32, 82; nonwords, 68, 156; overlay as, 6; sense and, 50, 75, 78, 79, 80, 81; unworded the, 76
World, 1, 2, 3, 70; human, 6, 12, 33, 34, 35, 106, 150, 184; inner, 4, 8, 12; outer, 4, 8, 11, 12, 17
Worth, 12, 15, 16, 30, 31, 35, 63, 154, 157, 158; vivial sense and, 82–4, 110, 126, 145, 150, 152, 156, 160, 182, 183

Zen, 73, 142